ENOUGH

Enough

Notes From a Woman
Who Has Finally Found It

Shauna M. Ahern

SASQUATCH BOOKS
SEATTLE

Printed in Canada

SASQUATCH BOOKS with colophon is a registered
trademark of Penguin Random House LLC

23 22 21 20 19   9 8 7 6 5 4 3 2 1

Editor: Susan Roxborough
Production editor: Jill Saginario
Cover design: Abby Weintraub
Design: Bryce de Flamand
Illustration credits: © iStockphoto.com I WEKWEK – Cosmetics design
elements (front cover, pgs iii, 17, 75, 161)

Library of Congress Cataloging-in-Publication Data
Names: Ahern, Shauna James, author.
Title: Enough : notes from a woman who has finally found it / by
    Shauna M. Ahern.
Description: Seattle : Sasquatch Books, [2019]
Identifiers: LCCN 2019003128 I ISBN 9781632172174 (hard cover)
Subjects: LCSH: Ahern, Shauna James--Anecdotes. I Self-acceptance in
    women. I Contentment.
Classification: LCC HQ1206 .H275 2019 I DDC 155.2--dc23
LC record available at https://lccn.loc.gov/2019003128

ISBN: 978-1-63217-217-4

Sasquatch Books
1904 Third Avenue, Suite 710
Seattle, WA 98101

SasquatchBooks.com

For Dr. G, whose gentle questions led to this book.

And for my parents, whom I know do love me.
I know now they did the best they could.

CONTENTS

I CAN'T FEEL THE LEFT
SIDE OF MY FACE

B efore I could say these words out loud, I stayed silent.
I tried to remind myself how to say anything coher-
ent. I practiced each sentence three times in my mind, stutter
stepping and stumbling over words that felt unfamiliar on
my tongue. *Numb. What does that mean?* I said the sentence
again, without saying it aloud. *Face?*

What is a face again? I reached up with my left hand to
feel the space between my ear and chin and found it gone. I
couldn't feel it at all. The left side of my tongue felt thicker
than normal. My head hurt when I tried to find the words
receding into shadows and grey garbles. If I didn't say it
soon, I might not talk again.

I cleared my throat and looked around the cooking
studio. "Is it weird that I can't feel the left side of my face?"

I remember my friend Trish's eyes darting at me fast. I
remember the way my EMT friend Ken put the palms of his
hands on the desk for a beat before he looked at me directly.

I remember how there was silence in the room, matching the silence in my head. Then Ken said, "Yes, it is."

• • •

That morning, I had woken up feeling off. My eyes felt as though they were bulging out of their sockets, especially my left one. *Is it possible to sleep the wrong way on your eye?* I wondered as soon as I woke up. My oldest, dearest friend in the world, Sharon, was staying at our house. She commiserated when I said I had a bad headache. I drank my third cup of coffee while she started her first. Everything had felt entangled lately—too many emails and bills to pay, too many meetings to hold. We were scrambling for money, again. But we had a possible deal with a company that wanted to make a bread with our recipe, using our logo, for the national market. Our next cookbook's publication day loomed, only three months away. We had opened our gluten-free flour company for business three months before, and we spent part of each day packing boxes of flour into larger boxes, then driving them to the post office uptown before five o'clock. Our six-year-old daughter and fifteen-month-old son deserved more of our attention. I woke up most nights, two or three or six times, circling items in our bank account in my mind, panicking at the gap I could see coming in a few weeks if something didn't change. Exercise? No time. My meditation practice? Mostly forgotten, except for two-minute sessions in the car between dropping off kids and reaching our cooking studio to start working.

I told as much of this to Sharon as I could, then cried in ugly spasms. She hugged me and patted my shoulder. For thirty years we had traded turns taking care of each other. It was my turn to be a mess. I collected myself after her kindness. I reminded myself what everyone said: *The first year of running your own business is hard. Everyone has been through this. Hold on.*

I noticed, though, how much I'd had to leave out of this jumbled story, because the words flew away from my brain before I could settle them down onto my tongue.

The morning had been tough. Trish was working with us to lift our nascent business into a thriving empire. But she seemed frustrated, since we couldn't seem to settle on the next five intellectual property deals we wanted to pursue. Ken had volunteered to work with us recently, since he was a whiz at Internet promotions. He chimed in on ideas for flour-packaging design.

Danny, my husband, had stayed mostly quiet, as he does. He takes in everything before he forms opinions. He doesn't feel the need to talk. He stood in the studio kitchen chopping carrots and prepping dishes we would be photographing that afternoon.

I sat at the table trying to pretend that everything was fine. *No problems here. I'll keep nodding.* Trish looked at me once in a while, probably confused as to why I wasn't talking. I rarely have a problem talking. She had told me, a couple of months before, "You are one of the most creative people I have ever met in my life." I'm not sure it was entirely a compliment, since she was referring to the dozen new ideas I discussed with her on a daily basis, my hands wildly gesticulating in the air, my words zooming around the room.

But I had no new ideas that day.

Danny said his see-you-soons to us all, since he needed to pick up our daughter from kindergarten. I noticed he had a full cup of hot coffee in his mason jar with a lid. Instead of waving and staying at the meeting, I stood up, awkwardly. I followed him outside to the car.

"Why didn't you make me coffee?" I stuttered at him angrily. He looked at me sideways, his eyes widening. We don't normally fight. I don't care about petty shit. I've been through enough to know that tiny fights about territory are normally about something else. But that morning, I couldn't see beyond it. I needed that coffee for my throbbing headache. Maybe coffee would help stop the weird tingling prickles at my temples.

He apologized and drove away, the dust kicking up from the back tires. I walked back in, slowly, noticing that my left leg felt weaker than it had when I woke up. And the left side of my face felt numb.

Instead of going back to the table, I hobbled into the bathroom. For a moment, I leaned against the counter, noticing that my left hip had started to feel numb too. The phone. I needed Google. I searched *Bell's palsy*, looking for an answer. Somehow I remembered that my mother had woken up one morning, many years before, with a droopy paralysis on one side of her face, her fear frozen on her. Had I repeated her experience, doomed to always deal with her? So I googled and found the symptoms: pain behind the ear, drooling, increased sensitivity to sound. The only thing I shared was the numbness in the face. And nowhere did it mention the creeping feeling of cold numbness spreading down to my arm now too.

I slowly walked back to the table from the bathroom, pausing a few times to make sure I didn't fall over. Instead of saying something, I pretended again. I heaved myself down in my chair and tried to form sentences. *I should say something. This isn't right. Ken will know.* But I didn't. I didn't say anything because I knew the sentences would come out wrong, all jumbled and dumb sounding. I didn't want to sound dumb.

By this time, the numbness covered the entire left side of my head and neck, went down my left arm, along my left side, into my hip, and was starting down my leg. I somehow sensed that I might lose the ability to speak at all, if I didn't speak now.

And so I asked Ken, "Is it weird that I can't feel the left side of my face?"

• • •

Let me give you a piece of advice. If you're going to have a medical emergency in the middle of a meeting, in a kitchen on a farm, on a rural island a ferry ride away from the closest hospital, be sure to have a volunteer firefighter on your team.

I still think of Ken's calm every day. He stood up immediately but without any panic. He walked over to me and asked me to hold up my arms. I saw him notice that my left arm drooped down at my side. He looked in my eyes and asked me to smile. It seemed impossible at the time. He stepped back and said, "Well, you're clearly having a neurological incident. Let's get you in."

And instead of relenting, grateful he was doing something about the fear slowly settling over my body, I protested.

"I can't be having a stroke. Can I? I mean . . ."

He nodded, then suggested going to the mainland.

"Danny can drive you to your doctor in Seattle. Or, if he drives you to the fire station here, they can do a few tests. If you need it, the ambulance ride is free."

Even in the fuzzy lint jelly that was becoming my mind, I heard that he understood me. Money had been such a concern lately, a pounding in the brain. Free ambulance ride?

Still. A stroke? I was only forty-eight. How could this be?

Ken, with kindness in his eyes, took a breath.

"Okay, I had a call recently. A woman who had suffered a stroke once before called us because she knew it was starting again. The only clues she had were that the top of her head tingled and her writing looked funny."

I swiveled, swaying, to the table. Writing. Writing has been the great fact and passion of my life, breath and body, hope and mundane daily scrawling. I don't quite understand anything until I have written about it. I sat down and grabbed a pen.

Slowly, the letters juttered out onto the paper beneath me. Desperate to prove Ken wrong, I pointed to the words on the page.

"See? That's not weird."

Ken nodded, then said, "Yes, but isn't it the left side of your body that's affected? Try writing with that hand."

My left hand skittered sideways, slowly, fumbling for the pen. As soon as I held it and tried to write a letter, I could feel the electric jolt of *wrong wrong wrong something is wrong*. I threw away the pen.

"Can you call Danny back here?" I asked.

•••

The next hour or two didn't really exist for me, so my memory moves like a montage.

Danny swinging my legs into the car. The swoop of the road up the west side of the island, so familiar to me, the fir trees blurring into a fast path of dark green and black against the sky. Rounding the curve that meant we were coming into town and knowing, in a moment of clarity: *That's it. I can't talk anymore.* Reaching my right hand out for Danny as he opened the car door in the parking lot of the fire station. Slumping against him as we walked, my left leg disappeared into numbness. *Why are they doing the tests in the ambulance?* I wondered as they lifted me in. Looking at Danny, his face terrified, and trying to beam *I love you I'm sure it will be fine* with my eyes, since I could no longer talk. The door of the ambulance closing him away from me.

The medics, merely kind bland faces to me at that point, put sensors and tubes all over me. Machines beeped. They placed an aspirin under my tongue. I heard the siren wail and looked out the window to see we were speeding out of town toward the ferry. *I hope everyone is okay*, I heard in my mind, instinctively repeating the phrase I taught my daughter to say whenever we saw an ambulance heading north. The medics talked to each other. I saw numbers light up on a little screen to my right. High. My chest started to hurt, a dull ache underneath my ribs growing sharp. Lots of questions. I nodded and grunted. I couldn't remember them.

And still I had my phone clutched in my right hand. It beeped, text messages coming in, and I raised the phone to my face to answer. I couldn't let them go unanswered. "Are you okay? Where are they taking you? Don't worry about the kids. We'll figure out someone to watch them. Where are you now?" Danny and Sharon were both texting me, the sound of the text tone rattling in my brain. I could hear monitors screeching.

When we stopped, waiting for the ferry that had been pulled back into the dock to let us on, I saw the tall older medic who had led me to the ambulance open the door and get in. Confused, I mustered up the word. "You?" Calm and sweeping his hands over my chest, he said, "I'm the one that comes when it's cardiac. I'm riding along with you, just to be sure." Cardiac? Heart attack too?

After the ambulance drove onto the ferry and parked in front, and I felt the familiar chug and push as the boat left the dock, I could feel something in me retreat. We were here, on our way to the hospital, everyone informed, every wire and sensor plugged in and working.

And I descended. I could feel my body slowly sinking into murky waters. I suppose I was drowning. But I wasn't scared. There was no visceral tug and thrashing. I merely sank down, down past the point of hearing anything on the surface. I felt held in the water, warm. I could feel that the water had a presence, that it parted to make way for me, heading toward the silty bottom. I didn't move my arms and legs. I kept my eyes open. I saw, far off in the distance now, the surface of the water, brighter than this yellowy grey at the bottom. Below me, I could feel the depths coming closer, slowly. And I looked up to the light at the top, little pinpricks diffusing over the surface. *I suppose I ought to go back up now,* I thought. *I guess I'm ready.* So I kicked, gently. My body knew what to do. There was no struggle.

I surfaced on the stretcher, being wheeled into the hospital. I remember how warm the air felt on my skin before we went in.

. . .

By the time they wheeled me into the little white room, I felt something returning. I asked the nurse what was happening to me, then noticed I had asked her a question. Out loud. Without thinking about the words. I was starting to talk again.

They rushed me into another room, eased my head into a giant CT machine and told me to breathe. Since I still couldn't move much of the left side of my body, I didn't flinch. They wheeled me back into the first room. Nurses talked to me in soothing voices. There were tests and pokes and questions in the corner of the room. I looked at my phone, still clutched in my right hand, and saw a text from Danny. He and Sharon were on their way. I drifted off, woke up to more tests, waited.

An older male doctor came into the room, patted my hand, and sat down. He explained that the CT scan suggested I was having a stroke. I gulped in air, then let it go. I mean, I knew. But still, a stroke? He asked me about when the first symptoms started, then told me it had been too long to give me the medicine they can administer right away to try to halt strokes. They needed another CT scan to look more specifically at the blood vessels in my brain.

"The best we can hope for now is that the symptoms start to dissipate on their own. You weren't talking before, right? And now I'm hearing questions and sentences from you.

That might suggest this is what we call a transient ischemic attack (TIA). It's a neurological event, which functions the same way as a stroke, with a blood clot blocking oxygen to the brain, but the clot breaks up on its own. We'll just have to see."

He patted my hand again and left the room.

I have always been fascinated by medicine. I wanted to be a pediatric oncologist when I was a teenager. Our daughter had been in the ICU the first week after she was born; she had also endured skull surgery at nine months old. I led us through the research, surviving the terror through fascination with the facts. Medical facts did not scare me.

The waiting scared me.

When Danny and Sharon walked through the door, they hugged me and I felt safe for a few moments. Slowly, I started telling them about the test, the doctor, the uncertainty. They listened. Sharon grabbed my right hand. Danny grabbed my left. Just as I noticed that I could feel his fingers in mine, he said, "Hey, wait a minute. You're talking."

There was hope.

Just as we were realizing this, a woman walked in with papers in her hand. Danny had given her my insurance card earlier. She handed it back to him, over my body, and said, "This didn't work. It looks like your insurance has lapsed. We'll need to bring you paperwork to set up a payment plan."

And then she left the room.

I could feel my entire body tense. The muscles in my chest started to ache in the familiar dance of shame and fear of not having enough money. Really? Was it necessary to tell a woman having a stroke that she would be bankrupt after all these tests?

I closed my eyes and said quietly to Danny, "We'll deal with it later."

• • •

The hospital moved me upstairs to a bed. Fragile as I felt, I could ask questions and move my left arm when they asked. I felt like I was gradually starting to come back to myself, like I was hobbling through a dark tunnel toward sunlight at the end. The young nurse on the stroke floor looked surprised to see me—two decades younger than everyone else there and moving my legs.

"I think you're going to be fine."

That made the room brighter for a few moments.

Danny and Sharon stayed with me for the next few hours. They left only to get dinner. I had urgently asked my husband to pick up a new phone charger while they were out. The battery on my phone was dwindling and I didn't want to be without it when they went home. They came back smelling of french fries and fresh air. Danny plugged in my phone. I was surprised to see an outlet on the side of the hospital bed.

Eventually, as the light waned outside, they said their goodbyes. By then I was able to talk normally. My face no longer felt numb. My left arm had returned. Only my left leg below the knee felt removed, but I could feel prickles in my thigh. It seemed I *was* going to be fine.

Danny cried when he hugged me. He was so relieved to hear my voice, clear. I held him for a moment, my left arm weak against his neck. Sharon hugged me hard. She and I had seen each other through some hard times. But this one had been the most terrifying.

And then I was alone in the room. Machines beeped. I could hear moans down the hallway. Nurses came in to take my vitals once in a while or offer me juice. But for the most part, I was alone.

Alone with my thoughts.

How the hell did I get here? What happened? How badly will this damage me? And how the hell are we going to pay for this?

• • •

In the middle of the night, a nurse woke me up to take my vitals. In the morning, I woke up exhausted. The nurse brought breakfast, which I mostly ignored. Food didn't seem to matter in that moment.

A young man wheeled in an echocardiogram machine to check on my heart. As the technician was rolling the sensor over my chest, he said, "Hey, so my girlfriend and I made one of your recipes for dinner last night. We're big fans."

I grimaced a bit, then smiled my practiced smile. "Oh, thank you. Of course. So glad you enjoy our work." Turns out I did not have a hole in my heart.

By the time Danny and Sharon returned, I had been cleared to leave. The mood was much lighter. Danny was back to fart jokes and teasing me. Physically, everything had returned.

Emotionally, spiritually, energywise? I was exhausted. Flattened. Terrified.

Still here.

Sharon hugged me on her way to her car to drive back to Portland. Danny held my hand after she left. We didn't talk much. He could see the sad terror in my eyes. After I signed discharge papers and changed back into my clothes from the day before, he guided me into a wheelchair, pushed me to the outside exit, then led me by the hand to the car. I was going home.

. . .

The next day, our doctor called me from his camping trip. Danny told me later he had been far out of cell phone range, backpacking with his family, on the day of my ministroke. When he had biked into town, he saw Danny's frantic messages, so he biked another eleven miles to a place with good cell reception and called me.

I talked to him, my words coming out slowly, as I sat on the front porch, the weak June sunlight pressing on my closed eyes. He listened as I repeated what had happened, a story I would tell so many times in the next few weeks, trying to understand it. Our doctor is more thoughtful than any person I have met. He gave a small *hmmm* as he listened to me. And then he said something that surprised me. "Shauna, all of your medical tests came back healthy. Your brain, your heart, your arteries—they're all in great shape."

Immediately, I worried that he doubted me. It really had happened.

He explained that sometimes a chunk of cholesterol in an otherwise healthy artery can break off and form a clot, blocking blood to the brain for a while. It can be random chance.

"But this is also a chance for you to think about your life, Shauna. We know that the tangible test results show that you're healthy. But what are the intangibles? Emotional stress on the body can cause physical damage. Stress can kill us. So what are the forces that have been causing you to lose sleep? To feel pain? To not take care of yourself? Where in your life do you not feel good enough?"

It was a question I pondered for months afterward, as I slowly regained my strength and mental clarity. It was the question that compelled me, over the next year, to start letting go of everything that didn't bring me joy. It was the question that I repeated to myself so many times it slowly became the only question that mattered.

It is the question that required me to write this book.

Why had I never felt like enough?

Not Good
Enough

FOLLOWING THE GIRL CODE

Hair

I honestly don't know why my mother gave me a home perm in 1976, the year I turned ten. Maybe it's because she gave my dad one first? Did my mother think that giving my father a "Mike Brady" perm, since so many men of the era had them, would make our family seem normal? (And did so many white men have home perms because they thought it made them look like they had Afros? Black men, finally able to let their hair go natural, then had to watch white men follow with temporary tight curls.)

I'm not sure I asked for that perm. But that would not have mattered then. I sat in a chair, my nose and eyes burning, as my mother squeezed pungent white liquid onto the rows of my hair shoved into pink curlers. I emerged with a tight tangle of curls, my thick hair stiffened into little ringlets that felt rigid against my ears. In my fifth-grade school photo I wore that perm, thick Coke-bottle glasses, and a plaid checked blouse that poofed at the waist. I was perched on a stool in front of the bicentennial flag. For years, I dreaded, absolutely dreaded, anyone ever seeing that photo.

At the beginning of seventh grade, when I tried so hard to make a hot curling iron feather my bangs, I burned my fingers instead. Most of high school I parted my hair down the middle, meticulously straight. I kept it short for years, in fluffy bobs or the "Dorothy Hamill" wedge, because when it was long it sat on my shoulders and drooped there. Never once did I have bouncy hair, Clairol hair, hair that swept around me in slow motion like the TV commercials told me I should have. Mostly, my hair was merely there. It made me feel weak, set apart from the standards of female beauty.

Eyes

When I was eight, a teacher noticed I was perpetually crinkling up my nose from squinting, my head jutted in front of my neck to see the board, even though I sat precisely in the first row. School test, then optometrist, and then I was told I needed glasses. My father tells me that when I put the thick glasses on my face, I looked around me and said, "Oh, so that's what the world looks like!" He and my mother felt horrible that I had been walking through the world seeing everything halfway, fuzzy. I was so glad to see.

At least once a year, though, my mother or father would say, "I know! Let's take a photograph of Shauna without her glasses." I'd pose, stiff and smile frozen, on the rocking chair with the wicker seat, and try to find them without squinting. My mother took out the Polaroid and we waited after the pop and release to see the film emerge from darkness.

There I was, vulnerable, not seeing. *Oh*, I'd think to myself. *So that's what I look like.*

Do you remember glasses in the 1970s? Mine were enormous, octagonal, and red rimmed. And my astigmatism was so bad that the lenses had to be as thick as an inch on a measuring stick. I lived in Los Angeles. I had a home perm, dark hair, a book in my hands at all times, and glasses that made me look like a nerd. Which, you know, I was. But a brunette bookworm with thick glasses in LA in the late '70s? Mortifying. I desperately wished I at least had normal eyes.

Cheeks

My cheeks are too chubby. Have you seen these? I'm a chipmunk with a glandular problem, all those acorns I'm storing for the winter balling up under my eyes.

Ears

My ears are all right. I guess.

Face

I have never known how to wear makeup. I've tried. I've put on eyeliner with little pencils, eye shadow with a sweep of the tiny brush that comes with the multipack of colors, and liquid eyeliner pens. It always smears. I cannot seem to spend the time in stillness required to make sure the colors shimmer perfectly on my lid. It always dissolves by the end of the day.

I get lipstick on my teeth, inevitably, and I have never found a shade that doesn't make me feel like a dog dressed up in a polka-dot dress with bright red lips. My eyelashes, once thick, are thinning now, and I need three coats of mascara to make them seem full, and then they look like shellacked spiders flapping on top of my eyes. My giant cheeks run to slapped red, so I should be applying foundation and powder to "even" out my skin, then adding a thin line of contouring pink-brown, right along my cheekbone. But foundation confuses me. I've never understood why I should paint my face a slightly different color, then pat with powder that also doesn't look like the color of my skin to look "finished."

I always feel like I'm preparing for my own funeral when I do a full face of makeup.

Jawline

For most of my life, my jawline has trembled with extra flesh. I have never seen my bone beneath my skin. Maybe if I ate fewer calories, I would achieve that dream—the jawline so defined I could see the shape of my skull when I grinned.

What I can see on my jawline, what has haunted me for years, is hair. Every morning I wake up with stubble, like a man. Dotted along my chin, down my neck, and above my lip, spiky little hairs grow quickly. I long ago lost count of how many times I have touched my face, running my fingers along my jaw to see if the hair has grown back too quickly, to feel comfortable in a social situation. I have ducked into bathrooms in friends' homes at parties where dinner has stretched so far into the evening that my five o'clock shadow looks like fuzzy grey lint has drifted to my chin. I have used their razors, quietly, turning the water on to the smallest drizzle so no one could hear me and then emerging into the living room, grateful everyone else drank too much wine to notice. Any time I slept over at a man's house, I waited until he collapsed into snoring after sex to put my feet onto the floor slowly, so as not to wake him. I tiptoed into the bathroom and dug into my purse to grab the disposable razor I put there for this purpose. I lathered up and shaved, trying to stave off the stubble until after we woke in the morning, after we kissed again, until I could get home and finally collapse, alone. Every time. And by five o'clock, I was shaving again.

Women aren't supposed to have facial hair. It's taboo. This, from a Spanish doctor in 1575: "Of course, the woman who has much body and facial hair (being of a more hot and dry nature) is also intelligent but disagreeable and argumentative, muscular, ugly, has a deep voice and frequent infertility problems."

So I have hidden what is plain on my face for decades now. I have tried Nair (burned my skin), plucking (left little pockmarks on my skin), and laser hair removal. That last form of removal, desperately expensive, seemed to do the trick for a bit. But then I met my husband and I got pregnant. After my daughter was born, the hormonal shift turned on me and my facial hair returned, even thicker this time. So I'm back to making sure I shave before I leave the house, keeping a razor tucked in my bag for days that go longer than I expected, and keep checking, furtively darting my fingers to my chin to make sure I still look normal, for the moment.

Collarbone

You know that hollow above the clavicle that models have, the triangle of air between the collarbone and shoulder, the carved-out emptiness of someone who doesn't overeat? I've never had that, not even as a child. Sometimes I dream of it, what it would look like to have a body so thin that my bones would be a fashion feature. Often, I have dreamed of it.

Arms

One evening, when I lived in New York City, I walked into a bodega on the Upper East Side with my friend Jill. She was a reporter for NY1, tiny and lithe, the way women are supposed to be. We were laughing as we reached for treats in the freezer. After a year of living in the city, away from the life I once knew as the only one to be true, I had started to grow more comfortable in myself. I was wearing a brown cap-sleeve t-shirt, my arms bare and swinging in the air. As we went to pay, the owner of the bodega, a tiny Chinese man, pointed at me and shouted, "Your arms! Too big!"

I looked at him, frozen as the Popsicle Firecracker in my left hand.

"Too big! You too big!" he shouted. "Like a man."

I had no idea what to say. Jill stayed silent too. I put the popsicle back into the chest freezer and walked out the door. Later that night, I threw out that shirt.

I have only rarely worn anything sleeveless: cute summer dresses, tank tops, swimsuits. Instead, I have spent my life finding thin sweaters and cover-ups for summer to wear on top of my short-sleeved shirts so my fleshy arms won't show. I have spent my life feeling that my arms were built for operating sledgehammers. They bulge out of short sleeves, as big as a man's. My forearms are muscular too. And when I was younger, they were covered in dark black hair so thick I shaved them at the beginning of every summer, enduring the itching when the hair started growing in for the sake of feeling like my arms were not embarrassing. But my upper arms? They were too much. Always too much.

Breasts

I sprouted breasts when I was ten. My parents never discussed puberty with me, so I had no idea what was happening. As my hips stretched open and my belly grew a curve, I was sure that I was growing fatter and put myself on a diet. My pubic hair appalled me, an abomination I had to keep to myself, since I was certain there must be something wrong with me. I sniffed under my arms, constantly, afraid that I must smell bad, too masculine. The night I first started my period, I ran out of the bathroom crying, telling my parents they had to take me to the hospital, since I was bleeding "down there." They looked at each other, then my mother said, "Well, I didn't think this was going to happen for a while so I didn't say anything."

She showed me how to use a sanitary belt and put on a pad and didn't explain much else that I remember. The next year, in school, the girls were shepherded into a room and watched a film about *menstruation*. Mostly, I remember a girl in a bikini sulking by the edge of the pool, finally explaining to someone that she "had the curse." By then, I had a bra full to bursting when all the other girls in my class were still flat. And already I had learned to curve my shoulders forward, like a bird trying to protect her babies in the nest. I have spent my life with my shoulders hunched, trying to pretend my breasts were not as big as they are.

By age twenty, my breasts were a 40GG. Essentially, I had *Real Housewives* post-surgery tits. I spent decades being regarded as a sexual object first, then someone with a brain. I grew so used to being ogled—on the streets of New York and London and Los Angeles—that I almost stopped registering it entirely. One day, in Rome, even a priest looked at my boobs first, then my face, and then kissed his fist and spread his fingers wide open. For most of my life, I have been a pair of boobs to most of the world.

They were too big. I have always wanted to have small, sweet breasts that sat on my chest, pert and waiting for attention. I cannot imagine what it would have been like to have no one notice my chest or for most of the male world to look in my eyes without drifting slowly downward. Huge breasts may sound great but they are, above all, an encumbrance. In the summer, they rest against your chest in the heat and you end up with a welted red rash underneath them, a yeast infection every July and August. Whenever I would try to run, my boobs would cross the finish line a beat before the rest of me. And without wearing three sports bras on top of each other, I would flop and bounce in a way that made me uncomfortable to be in public. It felt as though they were going to tear away from my skin. This made my body hard to be in.

Belly

Obviously my belly is too big. Obviously.

I started off a normal-looking kid. Not dainty. Never dainty. But I had legs that ran and arms that allowed me to talk with the air and a cute face with short hair and bright eyes. I was a kid. When I was about eight, after the dark time in my family began, I started to eat. And eat. I ate to stave off the sadness and anger I swallowed down and the unknown that made every moment electric for fear it might turn into a shouting match or questioning session or another night when I wasn't allowed to sleep. The only comfort, the only sure thing, was the taste of Twinkies or Ding Dongs or Dr Pepper or crisp bacon with that one little pocket of fat. I ate the food that lived in our home—a freezer full of frozen crisp chocolate and Abba-Zaba bars; a pantry full of cheesy crackers and Ruffles and jelly beans; a refrigerator with slices of individually wrapped American cheese and bologna and packages of biscuits ready to be baked and bottles of Coke and refrigerated cookie dough I could pop in my mouth any time I felt blue. And since this food was always in the house, and everyone in the house was eating it, no one asked why I was eating so much. Mostly, I'm guessing, because asking the question might open a can of something not so pleasant to digest. So we dived in for TV dinners and put spoons into jars of Cheez Whiz and ate Doritos right out of the bag. And it made me rounder, mostly in my belly. My belly started growing and it didn't stop for decades.

In my teens, I went to the doctor for a series of unexplained ailments. (Until I was diagnosed with celiac in my late thirties, I was always sick for one reason or another.) The doctor examined me and gasped when he saw the little bruises splattered across my lower abdomen like a Jackson Pollock painting in black and blue. He asked me about them, and I stammered that I didn't know why they appeared. He looked concerned, then his face furrowed into itself, the way doctors' faces do when they are equal parts curious and mad that they don't know the answer. I knew the answer. I had been doing this to myself. Determined to rid myself of fat, I had been finding little pea-sized pockets of fat and trying to burst them under my skin. I thought that the fat might float into my bloodstream and go away. Everything else had failed. I bought every magazine whose cover promised flat abs. I did curls and sit-ups and bicycle crunches in my room at night, before I would let myself sleep. I would put myself on crash diets of nothing but instant breakfast shakes until four o'clock, then eat a sensible salad and boneless skinless chicken. And even when I lost weight on the scale, my belly stayed round. So I thought I could pinch it away from myself. It didn't work.

My belly will never be small enough.

Legs

My thighs rub together, no space between them. When the heat goes above eighty degrees, as it often did in Los Angeles, and I had to wear shorts, my inner thighs chafed against each other until the skin was rubbed raw and red. And then I had to waddle into my house, trying to keep my legs far away from each other. I have never, ever had a thigh gap I wanted to show off in a swimsuit. Give me long pants every time. But I will still feel self-conscious that my thighs look more like sausages than slender pegs, the way every magazine my entire life has told me they should look.

I cannot cross my legs. I never have. My hips are too wide. Even with years of yoga, the most I can hope for is to deliberately perch one leg on top of the opposite knee, then keep them there by activating my groin muscles. After a while I grow exhausted and sit with both my feet on the floor instead. If I don't think about it enough, I will sit with my legs wide open, like some unaware guy on the New York subway, taking up three seats with the spread of his knees. It's probably because I didn't wear dresses, unless under duress for a family photo, until I was about sixteen. I never did learn to be demure.

I sprout hair on my legs overnight. Tufts of it grow at the top of my thighs, staying there most of the winter until the hair extends to halfway down my knee, and I shave it, reluctantly. When I was younger, I used to joke that I needed to shave below the knee every day, to make sure no one mistook me for a man dressing in drag.

Now that I'm a huge fan of *RuPaul's Drag Race*, I know that (a) no one would have mistaken me for one, but more like an awkward grown-up tomboy who is hirsute, and (b) honey, those queens make far better women than I do.

I seemed to cut myself shaving every third time. I still have a white scar near my ankle from the cut that wouldn't stop bleeding for most of a day. I'm hopeless at this.

Feet

I wear size ten shoes, in wide. I have peasant feet. Increasingly, as I grow older, they spread more. I'm down to combat boots, Birkenstocks, and comfortable shoes made for construction workers on their days off. And men's shoes. Mostly, I wear men's shoes. I never was very good at being a girl.

• • •

I have given a valedictorian speech in girl code. (I was always an overachiever.)

Girl code? *What's that?* Those of you who were girls in the United States in the late twentieth century probably know what I mean. This code has been written into us since birth, typed into us by television commercials and airbrushed photos and products on the market that insist we are not good enough as we are. Girl code is the unspoken rule that we must hate some part of our bodies fervently. We must say out loud what is wrong with us when we're in a group of girls. (*My hair? Oh, my hair is horrible. Look at your hair!*) Speaking in girl code is how we fit in. We must hunch our shoulders if we have large breasts. We must remove hair from all the "wrong" places. We must paint our faces to hide what we don't want anyone else to see. We must stoop down for a photograph if we're too tall. We have to know our best angles to make ourselves look thinner. (And this was long before cell phones and selfies.) Above all else, we must make ourselves small.

We must make ourselves small.

I WILL NEVER BE POPULAR

Elementary School

The day I began the fourth grade, my very traditional teacher told the class that she had one rule for PE. The girls would jump rope and the boys would play baseball. Every day, all year long. I hated jumping rope. It was a neat and tidy little activity for girls, who she thought were supposed to be dainty. (No one was going to be doing fierce double Dutch jumps on her watch.) The thought of standing in one cement space, underneath the awning so we wouldn't grow too tan—yes, she said this—made me ball my hands up into fists. Spontaneously, I raised one of those fists into the air to complain about this. She gave me the stink eye and said those were the rules. End of discussion.

But I couldn't sit with this. My fervent desire at the time was to be the first girl in the major leagues. (And write about it.) I used to sit in front of the television and watch Dodgers games, *with my glove on*. I couldn't leave the house much, due to my mom's fears, but I could stand in the backyard and throw myself pop-ups for hours. My heart pumped out Dodger blue blood, and my brain lived for the wonderful mix in baseball of technical strategy and the burst of breath that came from running to first base fast. This was my game. I needed to play.

My parents, who talked about current events with us at the dinner table, agreed. I had read about Title IX, which passed three years before. And I knew that Title IX stated: "No person in the United States shall, on the basis of sex, be excluded from participation in, be denied the benefits of, or be subjected to discrimination under any education program or activity receiving Federal financial assistance." I parsed out that sentence and made sure that my reading was right. The next day, I walked into the principal's office, put that sheet of paper on his desk, and declared, "My Title IX rights are being abrogated!"

I don't know how he suppressed his giggle. But he listened to me. And he informed the teacher that I was right.

She was never too fond of me after that.

I had won the right to play. However, the boys did not want me to play. I showed up for the first PE game. They told me I could be backstop catcher. That's the person who stands behind the catcher and picks up the balls that roll between his legs. No thanks. This was baseball, bigger than me. I told the boys, "Listen. Let me hit one time. If I get a hit, you let me play."

I hit a home run.

This was my moment, right? In the ABC Afterschool Specials, this is where everything turned and I became sort of cool to my classmates. Except, life is rarely like a fifty-minute TV movie that wraps up everything neatly. The boys let me play and fought over whose team I would be on every game after. But in class and on the playground, they ignored me. The girls in my class treated me like I was an alien. Why didn't I want to jump rope? Why was I trying to break the teacher's rules?

At least I had a baseball game a couple of times a week.

Every day in fifth grade I sat under a tree reading. Every few moments or so, I'd look up from my book to see my classmates running, playing handball against the big green wall. Clutches of girls would be gossiping, boys posturing, secret hand signals between them that felt like Mandarin to me. I didn't understand why the girls were so catty, the boys so slavishly devoted to the ones who ignored them the most obviously. People my age confused the hell out of me. So I read and read and read under that tree.

By the time I was eleven, my three favorite authors were Dorothy Parker, John Cheever, and W. Somerset Maugham.

It's not that I didn't want to join in. I did. I just sat to the side, watching, trying to decipher it all. British Victorian literature made more sense to me than this Southern California playground in 1976. I read more, hoping that someone would write out the key to the secret signals so I could decipher them.

One day, I was turning the corner toward our classroom when I heard someone say, "Hey, should we invite Shauna out there? She has boobs." I knew they were talking about the Out in the Woods Club, a name I had overheard in the whispers that floated over to me as I stared at my book. A select group of boys and girls would wander out to the eucalyptus trees at recess. It was rumored they kissed. Or touched each other. I didn't really want to go. But still, to be invited . . .

"Nah," I heard a familiar voice say. "She may have boobs but she's fat. Forget her."

That was Bobby P. He sat in front of me in class and I sent all my silent love and longing toward the back of his head. He had dazzling blue eyes and an ease with other people I never dreamed I would have. He was the most popular boy in class. And he had just called me fat and dismissed me out of hand.

I walked into the empty classroom, crying a bit. I often ducked in there early, to sit in the bean bag chair in the cool corner of the classroom, to find refuge against the inexplicable behavior of my classmates. This time, my teacher happened to be at her desk. She stood up when she saw me and said, "Shauna! I was just going to find you. I found out you have been chosen to represent our school on the district math team. Congratulations!"

I may have been fat, but I knew math.

(By the way, I wasn't fat. I see photographs of myself at the time and surge with rage for the way I held myself for years after hearing that comment. I hit puberty before anyone else in my class. I developed hips and a soft belly and breasts. That was it. But hearing Bobby say I was fat, and not having anyone to talk with about it, I began believing it. No fat girl is ever popular.)

• • •

A few days before we left elementary school for junior high, I stood on the risers in choir practice. At the time, I wore overalls to school every day, with a plain-colored t-shirt and some tennis shoes. Everything else seemed senseless. Overalls were good running clothes, sitting-on-the-ground clothes, tucking-one-leg-under-the-other-hip-while-concentrating-at-my-desk-during-quizzes clothes. Overalls also hid my burgeoning breasts, which were already too big. I didn't know yet that when you try to hide your body, you only draw more attention to it.

In the middle of class, a girl walked into the auditorium, slowly. The most popular girl in class was on crutches, with a sprained ankle, which had happened at recess the day before. Immediately, that high-pitched girl *Awww!* leaked out from everyone around me, the kind of sound usually reserved for pictures of puppies and small babies. The risers cleared as everyone gathered around her to make sure she was okay. Only the red-haired geeky boy with glasses and I remained standing on the stage, ready to go for one more rendition of "Joshua Fit the Battle of Jericho," our choir director's choice. We still had to practice the hand movements that accompanied our shouting of "Hallelujah! Hallelujah!" I watched this mass of sympathy and stood confused, again. A few minutes before, I had listened to three of those girls say conspicuously mean things about the girl on crutches. They were the first to rush to her side.

I stood there, rooted to the spot, unable to join the fray of girls faking it. I knew that day I would never be popular.

Junior High

In October of my seventh-grade year, I finally found a best friend. We watched every episode of *Monty Python's Flying Circus* we could manage to catch together. We memorized early Steve Martin records and recounted *Saturday Night Live* sketches when we next met. We played a lot of Boggle and chess, tossed the baseball in my backyard, and ate TV dinners in front of my television. We were instantly inseparable, bound to make each other laugh every time we were in the same room.

His name was Mike. And he epitomized late 1970s Southern California cool: blond hair that feathered back naturally, polo shirts, corduroys, Top-Siders. Every girl in the school wanted to be his girlfriend. Every one of them, as far as I could tell. So what the hell was he doing hanging out with me?

We understood each other. We had similar minds. We had both grown up reading a lot of books, watching a lot of films, and laughing at everything we could to stay afloat. I barely knew his family, since I never went to his house. He always came to mine. Once he told me that after his mother remarried, he never felt at home. His baby sister got all the attention. His stepfather had strict ideas about how Mike should grow to be a man. He wasn't happy there. I wasn't allowed to visit anyone else's home. But my parents loved Mike. They treated him like a second son, minus the fights and tirades that usually dominated our house in the afternoons and evenings. If Mike came over, we had a tentative peace balancing in the kitchen. For the first time in my life, I could start to breathe.

And then the phone calls began.

One night the phone rang around seven o'clock, just after dinner. I picked it up, thinking it was Mike with another silly reference, and I heard breathing, then cackling laughter. And then, a string of invectives against me. It was a group of girls, trying to disguise their voices. It sounded like they were talking through cones. I hung up the phone, in tears. And then I picked it up to listen for the dial tone and heard the same voices, menacing, telling me to stop talking to Mike. I hung up the phone. They were still there. Back then, the connection wouldn't go quiet until the one who had called hung up the phone. They kept the line open for at least half an hour.

They called our house every night for weeks.

I didn't tell my parents at first, because I didn't know what to do. But I rarely received phone calls, so it looked a bit suspicious when I stood twirling the curly cord in my fingers every evening. They got on the line, listened, and told the girls to stop.

"I'm going to tell your parents on you!" my mother shouted one time. But how? We had no idea who it was. It could have been any blonde girl at Emerson Junior High. And it just kept going and going.

I told Mike, eventually. He was mortified. He told me about one girl who kept pestering him, asking him to go to the school dance. But he was not allowed to attend dances, due to his family rules. So he brushed her off. And she had been making snide remarks to him ever since. Afterward, I hid behind a bathroom door and looked through the tiny gap between the door and the wall to watch my locker. I saw that girl and her two friends walk up, look around, and slip another hateful note inside it. They had been shoving notes in there for days. That confirmed who it was.

But what to do? I begged my parents not to tell my teachers or principal, since I knew that the girls would try to get back at me. So my dad came up with a plan. Just before seven one evening, the entire family gathered in the kitchen, with pots and pans, metal spoons, and drums. The phone rang.

My dad gave the cue. He picked it up and we started making noise. Lots and lots of noise, enough noise that pounding on pans started to feel good, a release against so much unhappiness in the house. My dad pointed to us to stop after a few moments, then he put his ear to the phone. There was a pause, and then he said, "Oh, hello Mary." It was my grandmother. He handed the phone to my mother to explain.

The next night, my dad checked to make sure it was the girls calling, then we repeated the noise. We shouted their names and told them to stop. They did. They never called back after that.

But I never felt as safe again. My friendship with Mike was tainted by it. He came around less often. Things came to a head when my mother grew angry because he never gave me a birthday present, and she called his mother to demand that Mike follow through on his promise. (I begged her not to do it.) He handed me a Steve Martin album but didn't look me in the eyes. We still made movies and hung out, just not the way we did before. And then I had to go and fall in love with him, a frisson that had never been part of our friendship before. I kissed him in front of the map of Disneyland in my room, and he kind of scrunched his nose up and backed out the door. We went to different high schools and only saw each other a couple of times more. And then he was gone.

High School

I set foot in Central Quad, tentatively, and then I stopped. This main square of my high school was enormous, a town square for teenagers. I started to sit down on a bench and unwrap my lunch, and a cheerleader glared at me. How was I to know that every bench was saved for a specific group of people? Four benches for cheerleaders: freshman, sophomore, junior, and senior. Four benches for football players, four for basketball players, four for jocks of all kinds. There were benches for girls with short skirts who knew how to wear makeup. There were benches for every different permutation of popular that existed in 1980 in Southern California. Why didn't they label the damned benches and save the rest of us the humiliation of daring to sit down on one? I retreated to the 400 Quad—where all the math classes were—to sit on a bench in front of my new locker. There, no one talked to me, but no one kicked me out.

I never imagined anymore that I would be popular. In a school of two thousand students, staying anonymous was actually an asset. I could slip between people and walk to my next class without worrying if they approved of how I looked. Because most of them never looked at me. I was a freshman nerd, newly wearing contacts. I studied hard and did well in my classes.

My sophomore year, a friend I had met in gymnastics class—where yes, I had once choreographed a floor routine to "Martha My Dear" by the Beatles, which should tell you exactly how hip I was in early '80s LA—took me to her locker to introduce me to her eighth-grade sister, who was visiting school for the day. Sharon stood before me, her glasses as thick as the bottoms of Coke bottles. She ducked her shoulder under a bit, too shy to talk much. But when I mentioned the Beatles, her eyes brightened. We started talking and stood there until long after the bell rang. I was never late to class! When she started high school the next year, we started spending every afternoon at my house, watching

David Letterman episodes I had recorded on the Betamax the night before. We ogled Paul McCartney's butt in *A Hard Day's Night*. We never stopped laughing. I had another best friend, so much like Mike had been before her, but without any of the sexual tension. I started to feel at ease in myself.

By my junior year, I had a little clutch of friends who were also readers and thinkers, definitely geeks instead of freaks. Sharon and I had started the Beatles Club (!), and at our first meeting eighty-five people showed up (!!). I was a member of the school's Academic Decathlon team, practicing one afternoon a week. I spent one long weekend at a competition with my teammates taking tests about art history, writing essays, and answering questions about L. Ron Hubbard's book *Dianetics*. Our school came in second place for all of Southern California. We joked that we lost to Beverly Hills High School because their parents probably owned the paintings we studied. After that competition, I joined the Knowledge Bowl team and competed with them.

On New Year's Eve 1988, midway through my senior year, I had five girlfriends over to spend the night. We blasted Prince's "1999" as loudly as my parents would allow it, changing the lyrics to 1989. We had long discussions over who was better: the Beatles or Bruce Springsteen. (Sorry, Barbara. I love Bruce more now than I did then, but I still say the Beatles.) Later in the spring, my younger brother suggested we start a band. I played the drums. He played guitar. Sharon played the flute. Haruko was on piano, since she had been classically trained in Japan. Barbara was on viola. Erica was on violin. Our band name was Rockin' Andy and His Five Fabulous Babes. We were possibly the worst band of all time.

High School (Part II)

In my third year of teaching high school, a student of mine came in asking for help with her essay. She was a strong student but always wanted a better grade. I understood. I remembered. She played soccer, won homecoming queen, and seemed to have a lot of friends. She was the teenager I wished I had been. At a certain point, as we began talking about her essay, she started to cry. When I patted her on the back and asked her why, she spluttered that she had been suffering lately.

"Everyone else has it together but me. I just doubt myself, all the time. Nothing comes easily to me, even if it seems that way. I'm just so tired. I wish I were [name of another popular student in the class] instead. I know she doesn't have these problems."

I took a deep breath, then reassured her. And told her that the other girl probably thought the same of her. She shook her head no. *No. I'm sure she has it figured out.*

After I calmed her down, she walked out of my classroom. Five minutes later, [name of popular student in her class] walked through the door, asked for help with her essay, and also broke down about how hard it was to pretend to have an easy life. "If only I could be [name of girl who had been in the classroom just before her], I would have a much better life."

It was a gift to be a high school teacher. Because if you don't have a chance to know teenagers after you have been one, then you don't realize how fragile they are. How they need the benches in Central Quad to be marked-out territory because everything else in life is so damned confusing. The star quarterback whose dad drinks too much, the valedictorian too shy to ask a girl to prom, the geeky kid mortified by his acne, the queen bee of the mean girls whose dad never pays attention to her and whose mom is perpetually on a strict diet—almost all of them are busy trying to cover their suffering.

I have spent my entire life standing against the wall at parties, listening in on conversations. For years, decades really, I thought that made me not good enough. Like T. S. Eliot's Prufrock, I took far too much time "to prepare a face to meet the faces that you meet."

The years of college were particularly lonely—I was required to live at home all five years. That's probably all I need to say about that experience. I kept hoping I would learn to be coquettish, to walk like a girl, to be a proper woman. To be popular. It never happened. I realize now what I couldn't know then. That everyone makes mistakes and tries on faces and learns to be at ease through a volume of confusing social experiences until they get a grasp on who they are. I had so few of those social interactions that I was perpetually confused.

Being sheltered from the storm left me weakened.

The boys who called me fat, the girls who prank called my house, the girls who glared at me when I tried to sit on their benches? Those kids were *young*. You can't know that when you are young too. Every one of them was stumbling along.

PICK ME! PICK ME!

The story goes like this.

One day, after my mother had read a book to me a dozen times, I grabbed the picture book from her hands and said, "I'll read it now."

And I did. I was two. She was so amazed by my abilities that she wrote the words for everything in our house on index cards and pasted them on the objects: door, table, couch, phone. I'm told that I was reading full sentences at three. By five, when I walked through the door of my kindergarten classroom, I read chapter books by myself.

This is how I came to be sitting on a stool, high above my fellow classmates sitting crisscross applesauce on the worn rug beneath me. I read the words of a story to them, pausing between pages to turn the book outward, slowly sweeping the book left to right across the crowd so they could see the pictures. My teacher was outside the classroom, as I remember, taking a coffee break.

My mother used to tell this story to people and say, "That's Shauna. She was a born teacher. It was stamped on her forehead."

It felt lonely, above everyone, different than them all. How I longed to be on the carpet, just another squirmy kid, like everyone else.

When I was in the fifth grade, my teacher—a dead ringer for Gerald Ford—didn't know what to do with me. In Southern California at the time, reading instruction meant having kids read glossy cards from the SRA reading kit. Each card contained a couple of paragraphs about a dull and productive topic: turbine engines, rivers of North America, cats. On the back, two or three reading comprehension questions. During reading period, we were supposed to grab the next card in the color-coded group we were tackling, read the text, then write out the reading comprehension questions. Instead of goofing off or throwing balled-up pieces of paper like other kids did, I dutifully did my work.

Sometime after Halloween, after racing through three to ten cards and answers each period, I brought my last piece of lined paper to my teacher. "I'm finished," I told him.

"What did you finish?" he asked me.

"I finished the box."

The box was his year's curriculum. He had nothing else for me to do. The next day, when I returned to class, he informed me I had to read the entire box again. I looked at him, gulping back the tears, not daring to make a fuss.

It only took me a month to do them all over again.

After that, he let me sit in the yellow bean bag chair in the corner during reading time. I could read any book I wanted. I tackled Shakespeare, Greek mythology, *Harriet the Spy*, and anything that interested me. Everything about books interested me.

On my report card at the end of the year, after all the As, there was a note from my teacher: "Shauna has read 125 books this year."

I wish that I could say the "gifted" program I was put into at that school allowed me to find my people and a respite of intellectual stimulation. Instead, I dreaded two o'clock each day, when the secretary came over the loud-speaker to say, "Will the Mentally Gifted Minors please go to the gymnasium?" I might as well have worn a Kick Me sign on my back. And when I would reach the gym, our butterfly-obsessed teacher would often send us out to the field next door to catch butterflies with nets and pin them to boards for her collection. I never could bear to pierce the body of a butterfly with a sharp pin and watch it shudder to its death.

You see, my parents needed my brother and me to be the best. We were smart. We still are. There's no doubt of it. But after my mother had our IQs tested by the school when we were in kindergarten, she used to sit us both on her knees and tell us, repeatedly, "You are the two smartest children in the world."

We would look at each other, then look at her. My brother would say, "Mom, come on. That can't be true." She would nod gravely. It was true.

"Mom," I would say, my voice a little trembly. "Somewhere in the world, there are children with higher IQs than ours."

Nope, she would shake her head. "You are the smartest children in the world. You're it."

(Side note: we definitely were not the smartest children in the world.)

She also liked to tell us we were the kindest children in the world too. But mostly, smartest. So smart.

Imagine that pressure.

Who wants to be the smartest ever? But she's your mom. And you want to believe your mom.

For years, I lived in that pressure. I had to do better than anyone in class. Every year, I chose the first row for my seat. And with every question, like Hermione Granger, my hand shot up in the air. *Pick me! Pick me!* I pleaded with my fingers outstretched. I knew the answer. Who I was, for decades, was formed by that pressure for perfection and pleasing, for getting the best grades in class and sitting in the front row, hand held high. *Am I right? Did I get it right? Yes. Next question.* That pressure was immense, mostly silent, and always, always there. It formed me, the way a glacier slowly carves out rock as it moves.

All through middle school, every class, I worked and studied and got straight As. Not one thing from any of my classes has stuck, because I wasn't in those classrooms. My body was there, with my hand stretched high, in science, in math, in English, in geography. Inside, my mind raced, replaying my parents' fights from the night before. Sometimes, their fighting kept me awake until deep into the night. The next morning, I was expected to wake up at the same time, get dressed, pack my backpack, and go to school to shine. I don't know how no teacher ever saw my tired eyes. But I probably didn't seem troubled to them. I always studied, always had the answers.

I had hopes for high school, for classes that would keep me thinking about anything besides the unhappiness at home and how lonely I felt. But in a high school with two thousand students, the percentage of incompetent teachers with tenure was pretty high. My freshman English teacher was an older hippie who also owned the town's natural foods store. Her class was in shambles. Sometimes she had us sit in a loopy circle on the floor and give back rubs to the person in front of us. She also, once a week, had us take turns giving compliments to each person in the room (including her). Several times a week she had us lie down on the floor while she played tapes with soothing sounds of the ocean and people whispering. I fell asleep every time. Somewhere in the year, this teacher grew mad that no one had turned in an assignment she had haphazardly given us a few weeks before. (Except for me, of course.) Suddenly indignant, she marched us down to the library and made us all check out copies of *Hamlet*. I felt gleeful. Finally! Work! We walked back to class and she angrily read out the first scene. When the bell rang, she demanded we read the first two acts that night. I did. When I returned to class, I found that she had forgotten her previous outburst. We gave each other back rubs. She never mentioned *Hamlet* again.

Inside me, every day in that class, I quivered. *How am I supposed to get a good grade on this shit?*

And through it all, I kept pumping out the As, one after another, in classes that meant nothing to me, for the most part. I plodded through them, mostly not having to study, but studying anyway because I didn't want to mess up. They all came easily to me: world geography, freshman biology, creative writing, European history. Bring it on. By my sophomore year, word must have gone around the teacher lounge that I was a good student, because I started getting good grades even when I didn't do good work. My chemistry teacher, another wacko, used to blow up potato bugs in the microwave in front of us. In one class, he threw a glass beaker on the floor and announced, "That will teach you to not walk barefoot in my class!" We were all wearing shoes. He made us do experiments without explaining them fully, then we had to write them up in our lab notebooks. Frustrated as hell that my garbled lab reports would come back with bright red As on the top, I once wrote in the middle of an equation: "You're not even reading this, you old fart, are you?" Another A.

Why did I worry? I wanted the A, right? By this time, I was being informed at home that I must bring home As because I had always done this and I needed to keep it up. But I wanted to learn. I loved the feeling of being absorbed in something, of discovery, of my brain firing up with new understandings. Hell, I really wasn't allowed to leave the house, so I had nothing else to do. I wanted to *learn*.

And then I took geometry.

Geometry never made sense to me. Algebra? Yes. But geometry? All those angles, the compasses, the neat lines, the unyielding truth of it. I couldn't find myself in its story. And this time, my teacher was paying attention to my homework. Every quiz and test came back with a B. Sometimes a B-plus. I freaked out. I had never received anything less than an A in my life. On anything. My mother kept asking me if I was doing my best. Why wasn't I spending more time on geometry homework? I did, more and more. And then I put away my homework for her Questions sessions, every night, after dinner. Sometimes, while she interrogated us about our days, asking whether or not we had seen any dogs or been kidnapped, I nodded in all the right places and went back to trying to figure out geometry in my head. At night, when I couldn't sleep, angles pounded in my brain. Why couldn't I crack this?

In the weeks before Christmas vacation, I started growing sick. I couldn't eat anymore. My stomach hurt. I started getting fevers. My mother, ever worried about my safety, rushed me to our family doctor. He was an older man with a thick German accent and gruff temperament. He prodded my abdomen and said we would need further tests.

"It could be ovarian cancer," he wondered aloud. All the way home, I cried and asked my parents if they would bring presents to the hospital. (Who the hell tells a fifteen-year-old she might have ovarian cancer?) It wasn't ovarian cancer or kidney failure or appendicitis. Finally, one set of doctors filled my intestines full of barium and x-rayed the length of them. In the middle of the tests, the doctors saw that my large intestine had a pronounced, contorted kink in it. They gave me some meditation tips and medication to help me relax. The doctors asked if there was anything at home that could be causing me such stress. My parents both shook their heads, baffled. (Baffled, I tell you. What could it have been?) By the end of Christmas break, I felt well enough to go back to school. I never could get my grade up past a B-plus. I never stopped worrying about it in my head.

Math Olympiad team. Olympic Decathlon. Knowledge Bowl. SAT star. Straight As, except for that one B-plus in geometry and an A-minus in trigonometry. It all led up to the big decision—where to go to college.

My entire life, I measured myself in grades and test scores. And so life seemed broken up into semesters and school breaks. I thought for sure that graduating high school and going to college would be the start of my life, away from my family. When I went away to college and lived in a dorm, flirted with boys and formed bonds that would last the rest of my life, I would be fine.

Everything in my life had been building up to this moment. College acceptance letters were the ultimate *Pick me! Pick me!* of my life. Early in my senior year, I had read in a big national news magazine that Stanford was the hardest college in the country to gain acceptance to. That was it. I loved an academic challenge. My parents encouraged me to apply, based on that magazine article. In fact, my mother insisted on rewriting my college application essay herself, after she read what I had written. She wanted it to be *great*.

To my amazement, I was accepted. In fact, my parents burst into my trigonometry class, brandishing the ripped-open envelope. I was the only student in my graduating class to get in. Validation. I was going to Stanford.

My parents told everyone they knew. When we were in Palo Alto, and stopped at a fast-food place for dinner, my dad told the kid working at the drive-through window at Burger King that we were there because I had been accepted to Stanford.

That first visitation day was possibly the best day of my life. I sat in on a freshman biology class and found I knew the answers to every question, thanks to the advanced anatomy and physiology class I had taken in high school, one of the few I had truly loved. A small psychology class fired up my brain. A junior-level literature class reminded me of the questions my favorite English teacher had asked us to consider when we read F. Scott Fitzgerald and e. e. cummings. I toured the freshman dorms, ate lunch at the cafeteria, and walked across the sunlit quad. It was finally happening. This would be my life. Only a few months from that day, I could start to breathe.

In the car with my family that evening, I babbled happily about everything I had seen. After a few moments, my mother turned to me from the front seat and said, "I don't like this area."

Confused, I stopped for a moment, then said, "What do you mean?"

"This town, this part of California. I don't like it," she said, derision in her voice.

Truly confused, I said, "Oh, well, I do. Sorry you don't."

She looked me in the eye as we waited at a stoplight and said, "You can't actually imagine that I'm going to let you go to college and not move the family to where you will be. I don't like this area." And she turned around to stare at the stoplight again.

Stunned, I sat in the darkness of the car. My brother was silent. My father said nothing. I looked out at the road with tears in my eyes. I didn't say anything before I went to bed that night in the hotel. I couldn't sleep for hours.

The next morning, I convinced myself that Stanford had been all wrong for me. The classes were too big. The people unfriendly. What a weird divide between the sciences and humanities, when I wanted to be in both worlds. It wasn't the right place for me.

I stuffed the screaming inside of me down deep, deep, deep.

So I went with plan B. We lived in a college town in Southern California. I would stay in our town, but I would live in the dorms. The local paper wrote a piece about how I had turned down Stanford to go to one of our fine colleges instead. I filled out all the paperwork. My parents sent in the deposit. I had the name of my college roommate.

And then my mother sat me down under a tree on campus. We had been touring the buildings, only a few weeks before school started. My father stood off to the side. My brother read a book under a different tree. And she explained to me that she was so disappointed with my selfishness. "By going to this school, you are making the family give up its dream."

My mother's family lived in Washington State. And she had this irrational dream that the family who always drove her crazy, the ones who compelled my parents to change their plane tickets and leave early every time we visited, the family who was cold and distant with her, would suddenly be close if we were in proximity. "You are making the family give up its dream" meant that my mother would have to stay in this college town so I could attend this place. If I chose to go to the small school in Washington, my third choice, my backup plan, then they would move to follow me. And my mother could be close to her family. *Why was I being so selfish?*

And so I gave in, just as I had with Stanford, because of her repeated threats of suicide, because of her cajoling, because of her constant reminding that her suffering was so much more than mine. I gave up that college too, even though I had an almost–full ride. At the last moment I enrolled at the small Washington school that was honored I had chosen them, but it had no money left for scholarships. My parents took out a student loan in my name and off we went. (FYI: Being close to my mother's family only made the fractious relationship worse.)

All the thinking I had done for decades, all the As, all the tests for which I had studied days in advance, all the papers I had typed, all the ideas I had investigated—they were not enough. They left me numb, in a U-Haul with my family, driving up Interstate 5 to start college in a place I didn't want to go.

College was a blur of learning and not much more. I loved my honors program in ancient Greek and Latin, with a study of intellectual history through the Enlightenment era. I studied the history of science and couldn't get enough of that. One semester of art history, psychology, English literature, and Greek tragedy classes, and I realized that the nuance and constant creativity of storytelling compelled me to keep studying the humanities, even though I had been sure I would become a doctor. (Whatever I had wanted to do as a kid—baseball player, environmental lawyer, doctor—I was always going to write about it.) Reading still thrilled me, especially now that I could read works by thinkers—Simone de Beauvoir and Jacques Lacan; John Stuart Mill and Ludwig Wittgenstein; Freud and Jung; Plato, Aristotle, and Socrates—and argue what they meant with other people who had actually read the books. I soaked up every word of Jane Austen, Charlotte Brontë, and George Eliot, thrilled that a curriculum finally included women writers. And let's be honest, I still raised my hand first most of the time.

But I was living at home with my parents, a thirty-minute drive from school, still obligated by my mother's suffering. "Just one more year," she told me year after year after year. "You know I can't do this yet. Why are you asking? Are you just trying to make me look bad?"

Mostly, in college, I went to class.

I got mostly As, except for the C-plus in Advanced Logic. The professor skipped an essential chapter and never seemed to care that we were all confused. This time, I didn't develop a hernia or a kink in my intestine. There was nowhere else to go. I had lost my drive to beat everyone else in class. I spent most of college depressed, I realize now.

A brilliant teacher inspired me to wake up. After I excelled in his comparative literature class, he asked me to join a little colloquium of students speaking about literature and philosophy in his office, a practice modeled on what he had learned at Oxford. He wanted to know my answers. More, he wanted to know my questions. Afterward, I returned home, barely acknowledged my parents, and spent nights in my room, reading and marking up texts, typing out papers beyond the ones required for classes, for the pure thrill of understanding. My professor encouraged me to keep writing, keep diving, keep mining my brain for more ideas. I did. I studied like it was my secret habit, my passion, and my way out. I started to care again.

Toward the end of my senior year, my professor encouraged me to apply for the most prestigious scholarship at my university, an all-expenses-paid yearlong trip of our own devising. We created our own curriculum for our year in the world, with an academic program and travel both. I researched and found literary journals in New York City, London, and Paris. I wrote to all the editors, as the editor of the literary journal and newspaper of my college, and asked if I could intern with them. They said yes. I researched places I could stay and intertwined my internships with studies of the history of small literary presses in the nineteenth century by planning to audit classes at NYU, the University of London, and the Sorbonne. I wrote reams of essays, a resume, and a written interview. After I made the final cut of applicants, I did a series of interviews in person with professors from my university and visiting professors. All of it I did in secret. I knew my mother would fake an aneurysm if I told her my plans. I needed to win that scholarship. This time, after college, finally I would be free to roam the world.

I came in second.

My professor called me to say he had voted for me to win the scholarship. But in the end, the committee chose the young man who was always my sparring partner and biggest competition in those evening office sessions. He was, also, my giant untold crush. Instantly, I hated him fiercely.

I told my parents that night. I told them, in no uncertain terms, that someone needed to go to the store and buy all the alcohol they could. My teetotaler mother was so relieved that she was seeing the terror of this situation through the lens of something that would not happen that she gave me what I wanted—my first raging drinking episode. (And my last. I was hungover for days. I didn't enjoy that at all.)

Instead of traveling through Europe on a budget the university gave me, I worked at a chain bookstore in the mall and lived in my parents' home the year after I graduated. Somehow, I almost had the courage to apply to NYU's MFA writing program. My mother found out when she saw the application in my desk drawer. She ripped it up.

I swallowed a bottle of pills that night.

And so I descended down, down, down, past the point where books could sustain me, past the point where I wrote words at all. I barely made it through that year, even after they pumped my stomach and suggested I try therapy. That didn't happen. My mother didn't believe in therapy. She wouldn't pay for it. And in my depression, the option of leaving the house, running away, paying my own way to Europe somehow? It never occurred to me. I didn't even know how to conceive that thought. I had always trusted my intellectual brain instead of my gut. My brother and I had been brainwashed by my parents to do whatever they wanted, since the damage done to Mom if we did something that would scare her was always so enormous that we couldn't see past it. We had it chanted to us, on my mother's knee: we were the smartest kids in the world. But we were also the kindest. And kind meant giving in to my mother's fears, instead of ever learning to listen to our own minds.

I was lost in the darkness in my parents' home, doomed to never date a man, doomed to be there forever. They had preached my genius to me, then told me I couldn't leave their sides. I could search every corner of my mind and write about it with solipsistic language. I could make every honor society for high grades and win the safe scholarships. But it was all for show. My parents groomed me for my intellect because they were the first in their families to graduate college and I was absolutely going to go. But college didn't help anything. It began to feel like I had worked that hard for good grades so I could be accepted to Stanford, solely so my parents could brag to the guy working the drive-through at Burger King.

My entire life, I had found my only sense of validation in the report cards printed on paper. Those grades could never represent the fear I felt that I would slip up, that I might not be the best, that I had to be the smartest, that I was miserable in the front row with my hand raised high. I never felt good enough.

At twenty-four, I realized that everything for which I had dedicated my life with a hyperfocus had led me to the darkest place of my life. I wanted to disappear.

I didn't think I wanted to exist.

I kept going.

I decided to get an MA in teaching. Getting a PhD in literature was also an option, until an English professor told me she hoped I made the right choice. "Public school teaching is such a white trash profession. You can do so much better." Nothing made me want to teach at a public high school more. And of course, the classroom was the only place I really understood. The program was at the same university where I had been an undergraduate. By this time my father had begun teaching there, so I was offered free tuition. I was still in my parents' home, but I sensed that with a career, I could save up enough money eventually to make a run for it. After a few classes, I realized I had found a home. And for the first time, I didn't care what grades I received. I wanted to teach.

I wanted to be one of the teachers who inspires students, who opens their minds to ideas they could take into their lives, who makes them laugh and makes them write and makes them feel alive. The three teachers in two decades who had made me feel like that were my guides. I didn't need to get the best grades to be that kind of teacher. I needed to pass through the master's program to reach a classroom.

I will always be grateful for those years I taught. I've been told by some of my former students that I changed their lives, that they know their minds better because I taught them. But mostly, they told me they could feel my humanity. They knew I chose to be there, whether I led them in a Beat poets coffeehouse reading, taught them how to read Willa Cather and Ken Kesey, or had them learn Greek and Latin roots and the parts of speech to consciously create the best sentences they could. I wanted them to share their stories and I wanted those stories to be clear. They told me they loved that I had them sit in a circle in the classroom. I never wanted a first row in my class. No one got to hide. What they learned mattered to me and I worked them *hard*. But one of the days I still remember best, almost twenty-five years later, is the day Kurt Cobain died. Those kids were shattered. We pushed the desks to the wall, threw away the day's plans, and sat on the floor to talk. They were humans before they were students.

Five years after I began teaching, I stood in the parking lot in front of my apartment with my dear friend Tita. She and I taught American studies together. She taught me how to be steady on my feet and trust my gut. Her friendship, and the fellowship I felt with my colleagues in teaching, had given me the courage to move out of my parents' home into that apartment on a rural island my second year as a teacher. Tita cheered me on when I had applied, the previous year, for a government grant to study Walt Whitman and Emily Dickinson at Columbia University for the summer. She didn't protest when I said, upon returning, that I had to leave teaching and move to New York. Tita understood why, symbolically, I had to apply to NYU for a master's in humanities—this time, on my own terms. We stood by my car as I loaded boxes into the trunk, to ship away, before I stepped on a plane the next day.

She hugged me and said, "You have changed so much in the last five years. You were so frightened when I first met you. And now, look at you. I always knew you had it in you. It has been such a gift to be your friend."

I hugged her, happy tears in my eyes this time. And when I pulled back, I looked at her and said, "Tita, you know me so well. What do you know about me ten years from now that I don't know yet?"

She paused and asked if I really wanted to hear. I did. She thought, and then said, "Ten years from now, your intellectualism won't matter to you at all."

It has been more than twenty years since that conversation. She was right.

THE FIRST TIME

In the corner of the room, the tilting, swirling room, my friend Sharon told me, "Go. You know you want to do it. You could get it over with tonight!"

I had pulled her over into the corner to ask her for advice. On one side of the dance floor stood an Irishman, charming and more than a little drunk. He had been plying me with compliments and Guinnesses all night, admiring the shape of my breasts moving in my shirt as I danced. And I had danced. Like a flower opening to the sun, I was unfurling in his gaze. He wanted me. Even I, usually so unable to read the signs, could tell that he wanted me. For more than an hour, he had been whispering in my ear. I had to bend down a little to hear him, as he was a couple of inches shorter than me. He was funny with shining eyes (increasingly dull after the drinks) and he wanted me. Why not?

On this side of the dance floor, however, I grew more sober as I wondered out loud to Sharon, "What should I do? I don't know him. He doesn't know me. This won't be about me. It will be about a quick lay." She urged me, having known me for more than fifteen years. Surely now was as good a time as any. Go. Get it over with.

I chewed on my fingernail, anxious to make the right decision. I adored how this man admired my body. It felt as though no one ever had before. But I couldn't do it. I couldn't be with someone obviously too drunk to recognize me in the morning. No booty call for me.

Quickly, I walked across the dance floor and gave him a little kiss, then gathered up my purse from the table and left the bar with Sharon. I was thirty-three years old and I was still a virgin.

• • •

I never intended to go that long into my life without sex. I never promised myself to God. I didn't wear a purity ring or chastity belt. My religion never dictated this. It just happened, over and over, through fear and shame, and then fear and shame of it having gone so long. The longer it went, the bigger it became. I hid the fact I was a virgin until well into my thirties from everyone but a few people. When I began therapy in New York, a quivering mess, I thought I was going there to deal with the fact that I didn't know how to let go and just get fucked. I faltered and stuttered through most of my first session, then I broke down and admitted, in a whisper, that I was past thirty and still a virgin.

My therapist said quietly, "You know, I have a client who is seventy-five and still a virgin." And then I roared, "I don't want that to be me!"

It took me a full year with that therapist before I began to understand. What led me there was only the surface symptom, the sprained ankle I complained about instead of the nagging knuckle of shame digging into my gut for most of my adult life. This was always about more than sex.

But why? Why did I wait until thirty-five to finally connect with a man and let him enter my body?

· · ·

The sound of shouting awoke me. I lay in the dark in my twin bed, my Dodgers cap hanging from the bedpost. In the stillness, I heard my parents' voices, yelling. I tensed up, a little feeling in my gut for the first time. Something was very wrong. They sounded ragged and filled with pain. Mostly, it was my mother's voice. She raged at my father, the floor shaking a little as she pounded her feet around the living room. I put my feet on the floor and hesitated. Should I go out there? Were they okay? My father talked a little, but my mother interrupted him every time. "I can't believe you're fucking . . . what the hell is wrong with you . . . what about our children . . . I don't want to be married to an adulterer . . ." That one caught my ear. What did that mean, adulterer? What did my father do? And then, as I crept out of bed and into the hallway, I heard her say, "You fucked her in a car in the parking lot. You didn't even have the decency to try to hide it." I had no idea what that meant, but I could feel it. I could feel the rage, the pain, the wrong. I put my head around the corner a bit. And on the wall of our living room, their shadows loomed enormous, dark against light, the two of them pacing and crossing each other. I headed into the living room to stop them, my tears already blurring my voice. When my father saw me, he stopped. He opened his mouth to say something and then I shouted with all my fury and fear, "You adulterer! You adulterer! You adulterer!"

I was seven.

A year later, my brother and I were sitting in front of our television in the den. My parents had already bathed us and dressed us for bed. They said, "There's a show we think you should watch." And then they sat in their tense silence, on either side of the couch, and didn't say a thing. The show was called *Where Did I Come From*, a cute cartoonish attempt to explain human biology. At the time, it was a breakthrough, since it showed adults in an anatomically correct fashion and used the real words of the body. *Penis. Vagina.* My mother had always told me to "be sure to wash your front bum" when I took a bath. She considered that better than the word her mother had used with her: "toony-woony." The show was based on a book, and the intention for broadcasting it on prime time was so parents could feel comfortable answering any questions. My parents, however, did not want to answer any questions. They both sat, arms crossed, and when the show was over, said tersely, "So. Is that clear?"

I had questions. I always had questions. When I was three, my father says he came into the den to find me with my head in my hands. When he asked me if I was okay, I looked up at him and said, "Does it ever stop?" I meant my brain. It never has. So yes, I had questions. But I took one look at their body posture and realized I wasn't going to be getting any answers here. I shook my head. My brother, who was only five, finally piped up. "I don't understand the part about the peanuts and pajamas!" We all laughed. It broke the tension. My mother explained the real names again, and then we got ready for bed.

Two years later, I finally told my mother I had more questions. I had been listening on the playground and some of it didn't make sense. Couldn't we please talk about this? She and my father set up an appointment for after school the next day. They sat on the couch, arms folded. "Go," they told me. "Ask your questions."

I took a breath and started with something I kept hearing other kids say. "What's a blow job?"

My mother took in a big breath, then set her face. "It's dirty and disgusting and you don't ever want to do it." And then she got up and walked away.

When my parents fought—and they fought every day, every afternoon, pacing around each other like animals going in for the kill—my mother brought it up every time. How my father's affairs destroyed her trust. How his need for sex was the death of our family. How vile and repugnant he was for doing this to her. How he should have contained his urges and put his pecker back in his pants. They did this daily, the same petulant, incompetent dance, and she said aloud it was all because of sex.

Like many girls in middle school, I swooned over cute boys and had posters on my walls of the ones I practiced loving by saying their names in the darkness. Shaun Cassidy! Mikhail Baryshnikov! Steve Martin! Paul McCartney! They were my stand-ins for the real men I imagined would come into my life later.

My freshman year in high school, I loved a boy who played basketball, a senior, impossibly tall, cute, and so far removed. I convinced my parents to take a different way home after evening events so we would pass his house and I could stare up at the lit bedroom window in the hopes of catching a glimpse of him. At the end of the year, I made myself walk up to him and ask him to sign my yearbook. I had never talked with him. He was, I swear, standing with the school's star quarterback at the time. They both looked at me and laughed, then walked away.

A couple of years later, a goofy boy who made me laugh at Academic Decathlon practices asked me to the prom. I could not believe my luck. I had never thought of him as kissing material, but he moved up to the top of the list. My mother was so excited that a boy wanted to take me to a dance that she took me shopping and bought me an expensive Laura Ashley dress. It hung draped over my closet door for days. I took it down after he called to say he had changed his mind. I was crushed.

And this was, of course, all standard stuff.

But through these times—Southern California in the mid-1980s—was a dark shadow spreading across the bleached concrete steps and the laughter of teenagers flirting. The AIDS crisis had entered the national consciousness. In my high school years, stories in the press were spreading fear of this new epidemic. My mother, driven by an irrational need for safety in all things, made it clear to me: do not have sex. You could die. Visions of Kaposi's sarcoma danced through my head when I thought about kissing a boy. I never spewed hatred about the men who were dying from this disease, the way she did. I also knew instinctively, from avid reading and my passion for science, that if I had used a condom with a high school boy in suburban California, my chances were pretty darned good for being safe. But still, my mother made it clear: do not have sex.

College was a series of crushes that never went anywhere. In one of my diaries at the time, I wrote breathlessly all summer about a boy I referred to as L. Maybe I was in a

Jane Austen phase? I have no idea now who L was. There was the earnest young man in lumberjack plaid who talked and talked with me about poetry and how to save the planet. One night, we stayed up talking in the college pub, drinking milkshakes, until far past the time I was supposed to be home. It felt meaningful, that conversation. I couldn't sleep that night, thinking about him. And the next day, I found out he had hooked up with another girl right after we talked and they were officially together. (He's married to her now. It's okay.) My senior year, there was a slippery kiss at a party where INXS was playing loudly and people were doing salt licks off each other's necks, then sucking on the limes in each other's teeth. This geeky guy I knew from logic class and I were standing off to the side, mortified, and then we looked at each other and sort of shrugged. It was my first kiss. It was cold and full of teeth.

Then there was the boy a couple of years younger than me whom I adored. His parents had become friends with my parents. So when he came back from college, I saw him sometimes. He was funny and sort of rugged and definitely a bit of a bad boy, in my eyes. (He had two girlfriends in one year and I thought that meant he played the field.) We bantered. A lot. Fact is, I had no idea how to flirt. I listened hard and asked people questions about their lives and talked about philosophy class and the meaning of life. I was so eager for friendship and human connection, and so desperate to be kissed, that I drank in every word spoken to me like elixir. So this boy—even though he seemed thrillingly like a man to me at the time—who played music, and possibly even smoked pot, seemed dangerous and tantalizing at the same time.

One Christmas vacation, he asked me to go to the movies. I had to negotiate this "date" for days. My mother never wanted me out of the house, beyond going back and forth to college classes. I never made the decision that I would be living at home. She told me. Normally, I wouldn't even ask, because I knew that anything out of the ordinary would send my mother into such a tizzy of panic and protective mechanisms to keep from feeling that panic that I didn't dare. But I knew she knew this boy, and his parents were her friends. So she let me go, under strict conditions. I had a curfew. And I had to find a phone to check in with her every hour. I agreed.

And that's why I thought it was a date, because the chance to go out to the movies with a guy and go out to eat afterward had never happened to me. I was twenty-one.

I thrilled in one moment during the movie when his arm brushed mine on the seat arm between us. But that, and the time he reached for popcorn and accidentally brushed my hand, was it. Afterward, he drove us to Dairy Queen, where we sat eating fries and soft serves. He told me about college for him, and quickly he confessed he was a little miserable. That he hooked up with girls, looking for connection, wondering when he would meet a girl with whom sex would mean something. He was starting to realize he was drinking too much. He was flailing a bit.

I don't know if it was his vulnerability that made me feel safe. Or if I was so desperate for someone to listen to me that I started talking. But I told him. I told him all about my family, the crazy lurking under the perfect exterior. How my parents seemed so great but they were broken and needing help. And I was flailing, a lot, because I still couldn't leave the house without being scrutinized, and my mother would not allow me to breathe. And the strict rules that made no sense. The fact that I had to go around to each window in their house and check, with both my parents, that the wooden dowels my mother had cut to the exact right size were in place in the window frame to make sure that no one could open the windows at night. I had to stand there, every night, at every window, and say, "Yes, Mom, it's closed." I had to jiggle the sliding window back and forth, several times, to show her, it's locked. *We're safe. You can sleep. Go to bed.*

He stared at me, mouth open, the hand with his fries frozen in midair.

And at that moment, the manager of the Dairy Queen said my name over the loudspeaker. I looked up from the table. My insides froze, then my gut started to burn and stab. I walked to the counter in a daze. And before I took the phone, I held it away from my ear, because I knew it was her. I had looked at the clock on my way up. I was ten minutes past the hour, ten minutes late in calling her. When I had been talking, for the first time about my family, my first time with anyone, she had been pacing the floor in our home, waiting for my call. She screamed at me through the phone, "Where are you? Come home right now." I handed the phone back to the employee and returned to the table. The boy looked away. We gathered our things. He drove me home. There was no goodnight kiss.

I never talked with him again.

I graduated college with honors but I wasn't allowed to leave home yet. Why? My mother told me I was her safety person, so the only way she could keep going every day, braving her fears one after another, checking to make sure the new bottle of ground cinnamon was tightly sealed, was to have me by her side. If I left, if I moved away, she would have to kill herself. And since I had been trained to take care of her since that night I chose her side by shouting "Adulterer!" at my dad, I knew nothing else. Of course I wasn't having sex. I was in my early twenties, living in my parents' house, spending every Saturday night drinking sodas and watching episodes of *COPS* with my folks.

I wrote. I wrote plenty of really terrible short stories, which I sent off to the *New Yorker* in a big batch, and felt wretched when they sent a form rejection letter without a note. But writing about this? About the wound I carried around that left me feeling crippled inside? No way.

For a while, I worked at a bookstore at the mall, near a military base. One day, a man who had just been transferred to the nearby army base came into the store looking for something. He decided it was me. We chatted. Mostly, I listened, as I always did. He came back the next day and asked me out for coffee. I met him at the coffee shop in the mall on my lunch break and he talked with his hands, excited, about the plans he had for his life. About halfway through, I realized he was a little too excited. There was something wild in his eyes, a frantic searching, an overactive certainty that he was going to change the world. He also didn't know much of anything about me, since he never asked about me. By the end of the coffee, I didn't feel comfortable telling him anything. He gave me a hug. I pulled away. I walked back to the bookstore.

The next day, he called me. I had given him my number when he first chatted me up in the bookstore. I didn't call him back. He started calling two to three times a day. My dad answered and told him I didn't want to talk to him. He demanded to hear it from me personally. So I got on the phone. He asked me where I had been. I had been subbing at that bookstore for another employee. My usual job was at a branch closer to my home. I told him that. He grew irate. "But after I figured out the days you worked, I changed my days off so we could have them together!" This scared the hell out of me and I got off the phone. He called back immediately. My dad answered and told the guy to stop calling. The guy started talking about how many guns he owned.

I quit my bookstore job that day.

· · ·

B ecoming a high school English teacher saved my mind. Everything before felt rooted in fear: *Pick me! I have the answer!* and *I'll never be good enough.* It had all been about me, but also not about me, since my mind was so intertwined with my mother's fears that I organized everything in my life around staving off her panic. Grading essays and leading discussions pulled me out of that tiny, tight space. I saw that I could be of use. I felt, for the first time, that I was someone.

Tita, the history teacher, and I began connecting over coffee in the staff room and started laughing right away. My second year of teaching she and I began team-teaching a class in American history and literature. By my fourth year there—after many dinners and walks on the beach, I began to trust her—I told her about my family and how crippled I felt. At the time, I was terrified, thinking she would reject me. Back then, I carried the shame of having been raised in a fucked-up family as though it were my fault. Tita, fourteen years older and so much wiser, listened. "How is this your fault?" She told me about other friends whom she had known with families like mine and how they had grown into themselves. We were walking on the beach as we talked, and in the moment I understood she still loved me. I could feel something in me break open and float away, over the water.

After I shared my story with Tita, I started to feel that I had spent decades with my vulnerable self tucked into a tiny box in my mind. Of course I had never been with a man. I had never let anyone see me naked because I didn't know how to be bare. After knowing that Tita loved me more after learning how much I had suffered, I realized I wanted to open wider. I wanted to stop pretending. And I wanted to be with someone, soon.

Still, I was a high school teacher on a rural island wearing flowery corduroy jumpers. I didn't like to drink in bars. I didn't want to date the parent of a student. Nearly thirty years old and I had no hope of any sex there.

So I moved to New York City, to open myself to more adventures, more people on the street, and the chance of meeting more men. I left teaching and found an apartment with two roommates on the Upper West Side. My dear friend Sharon lived in the city. The next year, she moved into my apartment when one of my roommates left. Our friend William moved into the third bedroom the next year, and we stayed up late talking nearly every night. We still refer to those years as our own little sitcom, 7B. And truly, fully, for the first time in my life, I felt alive. I took classes, tutored, wrote and wrote and wrote, started a screenplay-editing business, stayed up until four in the morning dancing, went to gay clubs with friends, did yoga, shopped at farmers' markets, made dozens of new friends, and walked around the city, entirely free. The person I am now was born in that city, born of my decision to free myself and start anew.

However, it turned out that Manhattan wasn't a much easier place to meet men than a rural island on the West Coast. I didn't understand the East Coast sensibility—at every party, the first question to me was, "Where did you go to school?"—and I didn't fit in. By then, I *really* didn't know how to have a normal conversation, to flirt, or to tell if a man liked me. I did go to an early online-dating café, where people filled out pages for a profile, the employees turned them into online pages, and people could drink coffee and drift through possibilities on a clunky computer.

I had a few dates with men that way. I connected with one man through that service who seemed interested. We met up at a bar in the middle of a snowstorm, then went back to his apartment to make out and dry hump for a while. But that was it. Every time it didn't work, I blamed myself. I was too intellectual or too fat or too safe or something. I mean, really. A thirty-something virgin in New York City? What chance did I have?

Through therapy and a lot of conversations, I realized that the desperation oozed out of me. I knew nothing about how to be with a man other than what I had seen in movies. The longer it went, the more I keened for something real. The longer it went, the more I wanted my first time to *mean* something.

In the meantime, I had girlfriends. The few women I shared this terrible secret with guided me in the right direction. I asked a lot of questions. I read everything about sex I could get my hands on and asked questions of anyone who would listen. I listened to my girlfriends talk about bad sex with lousy boyfriends. I listened to my male friends talk about the women they didn't want to date. I taught myself how to put a condom on a cucumber. And I masturbated, a lot, with slippery fingers and detachable showerheads, and then my first vibrator. I had started masturbating early, when I was a kid, but then I had felt guilty. Now, in New York City, in my thirties and finally free, I started giving myself as much pleasure as I wanted. And I wanted a lot of pleasure.

By the time I left New York to move back to Seattle, I knew how to satisfy myself. I returned to Seattle determined to start fresh. I knew, in my bones, that Seattle was where I would meet my husband. Somehow, I knew. And I also knew I didn't want the man I married to be the only person with whom I ever had sex. This was just after September 11, and the whole world felt ruptured. Fuck these purity tests. I just wanted to get laid.

And then it happened, with a man newly divorced and probably as intent on passing through to the other side as I was. Fact is, when he collapsed on top of me after some vigorous pushing, with the blankets over us, I couldn't tell if he had orgasmed. My orgasms with my vivid-pink ana-tomically correct vibrator (except for the slender attachment meant to stimulate the clitoris that had nothing to do with the male body) were far more explosive. By myself, I did a much better job than this experience had given me. I lay in the dark as he lay snoring beside me and thought, *Is that it? I mean, yay! I'm no longer a virgin. But really? That's it?*

That man and I had perfectly fine sex twice a week for about six weeks. When he broke up with me, I met a physics professor who was scared of his own body. That sex was not fun. After that, a few different one-night stands—always with a condom—some bumping and grinding, getting our rocks off. All of it was pretty tame. And after the big moment was done, I was pretty bored.

Seriously, that was it?

A couple of years later, I was sick as a dog for months, no one knowing what caused me such pain and exhaustion. When I was diagnosed with celiac, and told I had to give up gluten, I started to heal. And once I realized what had been plaguing me most of my life—causing stomachaches, repeated bouts of pneumonia, achy joints, and some long-term depression—I realized that I needed to stop trying to date. At thirty-eight years old, I was no longer a virgin, thank goodness. And because of that, I realized that it was never about the thrusting of an erect member into an orifice in my body. It was connection that I wanted. It was about being with someone who truly wanted to be with me.

I wanted to be with me. After years of therapy, meditation retreats, teaching, living in New York, making lifelong friends, and being honest with myself about my life? I was a self I had never known before. I wanted to stop searching. I vowed to not date anyone for a year. If someone was going to enter my body, he was going to have to deserve it.

Four days shy of that year, I met the man who would become my husband. He was the surprise of my life. I made him swear we wouldn't have sex for a few months, to be sure he really wanted me, even though we couldn't stop kissing. We didn't make it that far. The first time we were together, we went through an entire box of condoms and didn't sleep. We were inexhaustible. Within the first few moments of being naked with each other, it felt as though we were both truly there, bare, no pretending.

Enough
Pretending

THE F-WORDS

And should anyone be surprised

if sometimes, when the white moon rises,
women want to lash out
with a cutting edge?

—MARY OLIVER

• • •

Fuck

I love saying the word *fuck*. **FUCK.** It's sharp and guttural
and sometimes the only word—the *only word*, I tell you—
that makes any sense at all. Sometimes I say it in anger. *That
putz is such a fucking schmuck. What the fuck was he thinking of
when he said that? That's the fucking best they can do?* Sometimes
I say it in a long exhalation of pleasure. *Fuuuuuuuuck.* And
when I'm angry—righteously raging, not annoyed or irri-
tated but *angry*—it lands between every third word in my
sentences, in a monologue that would put a David Mamet
play to rest behind a preschool book in the library.

I know. I'm a woman. I'm supposed to be demure, aware of the effect of my language on any children nearby. You know what that directive is? *Be quiet. Stop talking. Say it nicer. You should try smiling sometimes. Really, the children.* Fuck that shit.

When the first cookbook my husband and I wrote was published, I was still naive enough to rush over to Amazon to see if there were any reviews. *Please love my work. Please tell me I'm going to be okay.* The first review, the only review, was from a woman who was outraged that she had bought the book and was reading it to her seven-year-old and read the word *fuck* in one of my essays. Outraged, I tell you! Immediately, I was mortified. So was our book editor, who wrote to say that we had to do something about this. I took to all the social media, letting people know that there is a swear word in the book and they should be warned. Many people wrote that it didn't bother them. Some of them wrote what I wanted to write: *Lady, what in the hell are you doing reading a narrative cookbook about a writer and a chef falling in love through food to a seven-year-old? Have you ever met a chef? Do you have any idea how much restraint it took to only use FUCK once?! And can you not read ahead and see that word coming and not read it if you are so concerned? Oh for fuck's sake.* But I couldn't write that. I had a book to sell. I had to make nice. And I was astonished to see how many people—all of them women—wrote that they would never be able to buy our book now. They had so been looking forward to the bread recipe, but they could not pay any money for a book that contained a terrible word like that.

Ladies, repeat after me: Fuck. FUCK. *FUCK.* **FUCK.**

If you haven't said that word once, that also means you have never accessed your rage.

And rage is useful. Rage is necessary. Rage is clean and clear, the first step toward breaking through, out of the box, into the open air.

Feminism

When I was in college, I found Simone de Beauvoir's book *The Second Sex*. I fell into the pages, ripping through them with increasingly awake anger. This book, published in 1949, felt like it was enormously alive, the words alert and tilted toward the times I lived in forty years after its publication. Everything she wrote about the subjugation of women felt like a truth I had known in my body but had never been able to articulate. I underlined nearly the entire book, the ink from my red pen bleeding onto the pages behind it, sometimes obscuring the words, making me read harder. When I reached this line, I circled it twenty times: "Her wings are cut and then she is blamed for not knowing how to fly."

This described what had happened to me, all through my life. It's what my mother and father had done to me, both of them, equally, through their obdurate insistence on pretending that everything was fine when we were dying inside that house. All the windows were shut tight. The door was nailed closed. And my wings were clipped, down to the nubs, so I could never question what was being done to me and fly away.

But I also knew, with the sudden, much broader perspective that one can only gain by flying high above the earth in warm air, that this was not my story alone. I felt the power of this sentence in my gut and understood it was my story and so many women's stories. It was the story of all marginalized people: of black women, and queer men, and anyone who is not Christian in America, and refugees, and those who are disabled, and those who cannot speak. It is the planned policy of those who are in power to keep others from realizing their own power. Clip their wings, then blame them for not knowing how to fly.

I looked up from the book with furious tears in my eyes.

And from that day forward, I called myself a feminist.

My mother scowled at me when I told her I was a feminist. She went into a long diatribe about "Oh, all those women who burned their bras and flounced off to protests in their long hippie skirts while the rest of us were doing the real work of the world, keeping house and raising children." These were familiar tropes, things she said so often I could have spit them back at her. Instead, I brought up intellectual arguments, quotes from the book, impassioned speeches. She waved her hand and laughed.

I wasn't brave enough to repeat back that quote that broke me open. I didn't know that it had yet. I just knew something had shifted.

Still, over the next ten years or so, I drifted back. I no longer believed my parents' version of the 1960s. But I hesitated before I called myself a feminist. If anyone asked, I said, "I'm a humanist. I believe in trying to lift up everyone. I don't want to say women are more important than men."

Oh god, *all lives matter* much?

Fact is, I had to liberate myself, with years of therapy, meditation retreats, and honest conversations with people who mattered to me most before I could see it clearly. Those clipped wings took decades to grow back. It's easier to make nice and say I want to work for everyone's freedom than to demand the liberation of women. Fact is, women have always been defined through men, the same way blackness has always been defined through whiteness, and homosexuality through heteronormativity. Unless we stand up and shout, "Nope. My turn. We're going to talk about me and my people now," then we will never learn to fly. It took me decades of working on myself before I could figure out my own shit and start truly turning to other people's liberation. The same will be true for us as a society.

I don't think we're going to see any real change in this culture until we put black women in charge of everything for at least fifty years.

In the meantime, the least I could do—and I do mean the *very least*—is to say it loudly. Fuck yes, I'm a feminist.

Fame

I once lived with a famous person in another famous person's house. I won't tell you anything identifying about this famous person because (1) I signed a nondisclosure form before I could move into my bedroom, and (2) this person's specific name and identity don't matter to this story. This is a story about fame, a fickle and ridiculous place to live.

(My husband would immediately like to tell you I was not *living* with this person, in that sense of the phrase. I was the privately hired book editor for Famous Person's romantic partner. The book was never published.)

Everything on the outside seemed perfect. We were living in an opulent house with an enormous kitchen, masseuses coming in every night to give a massage to Famous Person (whom I will now call FP), nannies, limousine drivers, personal chefs, risotto with truffle oil on demand, unlimited bank accounts with a team of accountants to keep track of it all and pay the bills, housekeepers, Italian silk sheets on the bed in the master bedroom, and adoring employees. It was the living embodiment of what so many Americans dream their lives will one day be like, if they make a video that goes viral or work on their singing career. This was the American dream come to fruition, right in front of me.

And it was empty. That house was a tight little box where almost everyone was doing one thing: keeping FP happy. Problem is, FP was never happy. FP was stoned, all the time, first thing in the morning to last thing at night. FP needed more and more and more, including having those Italian silk sheets changed every day because FP deserved clean sheets every night. (The monthly dry-cleaning bill was $11,000.) FP enjoyed family time but not taking care of their own child. That was the nanny's job. And whenever a new work debuted, just before the public saw it, FP was given a personal screening/listen/debut with only FP's family and friends. Afterward, for days, FP sat on the couch with head in hands, desolate, because they felt sure they were not good enough.

Once, I walked up to FP, put my hand on their arm, and listened as they talked about how hard this was, how they felt like a fake, how they were sure this time the public would see that behind the false front was a terrible artist. I listened for a long time and gave FP a reassuring talk and hug. The next time it happened, I put my hand on FP's arm and listened to the same spiel. I gave another hug. The third time it happened, I put my hand on FP's arm and said, "FP, you do this every time, the same speech, the same head in hands, the same three-day period of mourning on the couch. And it seems like it's a way to make sure that everyone swarms around you, reassuring you, making everything about you.

Did you ever think that this might be the problem?" FP looked up at me, astonished.

And it occurred to me that no one had told FP the truth in years. Everyone around FP was so eager to be near the glow of fame and money that they had given up the chance to connect with this person. To be real. And so around FP were crowds of people eager for an autograph, another chance to become rich, a clutch of people who would never tell FP the straight story. No wonder FP was so insecure. FP never did a thing. No cooking food or doing dishes, no driving or deciding how to spend money when the bank account was low, no mowing the lawn or taking out the trash or changing a baby's diaper, no chores or hard talks or saying no to desires, ever. FP was so swaddled in the soft cloth of people eager to leach off them that they might as well have not existed.

It's no way to live.

Fat

I'm fat. There's no getting around it. I'm FAT.

I have flesh under my chin, curves of flesh over my hips, muscles in my arms that are covered by flesh that sags, flesh upon flesh upon flesh on my belly that sometimes rolls when I turn over in bed, flesh on my thighs that dimples and puckers, and flesh on my ample fleshy butt. I'm fat.

There are so many names I have used in place of fat: *plump, curvy, big-boned, thick, husky, plus-size, big*. They were all names that sound more pleasing. *Fat* sounds like an insult. It has the guttural, short, sharp sound of *shit* and *fuck* and *dick*. It sounds like a slap on the cheek, in an empty room, unexpected.

And for years and years, I feared it. I would not allow myself to be fat. I couldn't be fat. I couldn't be a fat woman, singing a sad song.

Once, I read a book to my daughter, who was only two, and I skipped the word, when the writer in a silly sing-song described one thin man and one fat man. I didn't even want her to hear the word. I censored it for her so she wouldn't think of me as fat. Or herself, someday.

But then, I reached the age of no more pretending. No more fucks to give. All those years of hiding and using euphemisms and pretending that I was anything other than who I am—I sigh when I think of all that time. And I realized I had been so afraid of the word that I forgot to own it. How could there be room for all of me, this enormous panoply of stories and lives I have lived, the ways I have changed, the laughter bubbling up inside of me, the trauma I hold in my body, the love I live every day when I do the dishes and talk with my husband, and the many great meals he makes for me and our children, his love on a plate. My body is mine. I am here. I take up room. And my mother looks like I do, and her mother before her, and her mother before. We are ample women, strong as oxen, built like peasants who carry the world on their shoulders and birth babies and take up space in the world. This is who I am.

To employ a phrase from the great Walt Whitman: "I am large, I contain multitudes."

And so I'm not afraid of the word anymore. By every single narrow-minded definition of the word, I am fat. And I am here.

Call me fat. I am. You can't hurt me with that word anymore.

So when my son, who was only two, once said to me, "Mama, you have a fat belly," I smiled and rubbed my ample flesh, and said, "I know! I do. Isn't it beautiful?" And he nodded and curled up on me and hugged my belly with his body.

And I was home, unafraid, fat, and happy.

Fierce

There is no more pabulum word in the English language than *nice*.

This culture trains women to be nice. "You should smile more often," men say to women as they pass them on the street, reminding them that their place in this world is decoration. The next time I hear that, I think I might step in, look him in the eye, and say, "She doesn't owe you anything, asshole," then walk away.

In my teens and twenties and almost all through my thirties, I was nice. So very nice. I made sure to always hold doors, bring everyone I barely knew homemade muffins, and ask if I could do anything to help. I said "I'm sorry" automatically as I walked down the aisles of the grocery store and accidentally brushed my cart against someone else's. I had been trained since birth to not ask for much for myself, so even the slightest transgression blared in my mind like an angry child throwing a temper tantrum. *DO BETTER! WHAT IS WRONG WITH YOU?* And all this yelling for forgetting to say "Excuse me" before I walked behind someone in a library. In my mind, the only thing that mattered was being nice.

But nice doesn't change much in the world. Look, I believe in politeness. I have taught my children to say please and thank you. But I also have told them that they should say please because they are asking someone to stop what they are doing and change course for them. Please and thank you are a way of acknowledging that we're connected, that my actions affect yours, that we can recognize the other's basic goodness through a moment of gratitude. That's a hell of a lot different than nice.

Nice? Nice is suburban American women voting for a monster because their families have always voted for that political party and they don't want to make waves. Nice is looking the other way while neighbors pour milk over the heads of black folks sitting at a lunch counter in protest. Nice is not asking questions about the smoke coming from the German army barracks down the road. Nice is not wanting to discuss racism and saying, "Oh, I don't even see color! Everyone is the same to me." (Yeah, that's racist. You do see color. You just don't want to talk about it because it makes you uncomfortable.) Nice is indifference to everything but surface and the superficial. Nice is a fucking waste of time. It's also why all the world's atrocities have happened, because not enough people have been sufficiently horrified to speak up in front of their neighbors and make good trouble.

I don't want to be nice. I want to be *fierce*.

I take my cue from drag queens. These men dare to bend every gender norm by embodying this culture's feminine ideal of beauty, all while tucking their penises up with duct tape. There is nothing more incredible to me than a six-feet-four Puerto Rican man dressed in a cinched-in pink bustier with lavender flowers sprouting at the neckline, fishnet stockings, and a pair of six-inch stilettos. As RuPaul says, "We're all born naked and the rest is drag." And that's what I love about drag queens so much. They know they're pretending.

A fierce drag queen makes you interrogate gender, wrestle with the questions of why we find some qualities in women sexy and others not, and laugh your ass off while also being amazed at their death drops.

Most humans are walking around pretending all day long, pretending that they like their jobs, their spouses, their lot in life. We pretend that getting that new car will really make a difference in our lives. It doesn't. And within a month, we look for something else new. Drag queens? They're some of the most marginalized people in this culture and they're celebrating it with '80s pop songs and faces beat for the gods. (That last one is a good thing. Look it up.) Drag queens spend their time pretending to make you think about the way you pretend. They are fierce.

I remember a conversation I had years ago with a young gay man, a former student of mine. I took him to his first gay club when we lived in New York. He never did try drag but he loved it too. And he told me his definition of beauty: "Every one of us is beautiful because we're alive. We all have that potential. But some people just seem dead in the eyes. I think a person is truly beautiful when he or she lives in every part of their body, even down to their fingertips. That's beauty."

That's fierce.

Fudge

I'm not a fan.

It's too sweet. It's like pretend candy. And there's only one depth of flavor to it: sweet imitation chocolate. No thanks.

Besides, it will never be a satisfying substitute for the word *fuck*.

I MUST HAVE KILLED MY GRANDMOTHER FOUR HUNDRED TIMES

I must have killed my grandmother four hundred times before I entered the ninth grade.

It's not that I had any particular animus toward my grandmother. Sure, she was crabby and pretty selfish and not one bit kind. However, I saw her infrequently, once or twice a year, when my family and I flew up from Los Angeles to Seattle for a visit. Every time, the trips ended with my parents changing their tickets for a flight days earlier than they had originally booked. My mother wanted so badly to have a good relationship with her difficult family that she pretended to herself every few months that she loved them. She tried. Oh, she tried hard to be a dutiful daughter, to feel like they had the Norman Rockwell family of her childlike dreams. Instead, there were tears in the evening, silence at breakfast, nasty comments between my mother and her mother in the kitchen while we hid in the bedroom, lilting voices pretending to be at peace when the fight ended with no real resolution, and finally a giant blowout fight that resulted in us running to our rooms to pack our bags. My grandfather drove us to Sea-Tac airport in the early morning before he went to work, the entire car silent in the predawn darkness except for my mother's sniffles. I was so happy to get back on that plane, every time.

I killed my grandmother in words for the sake of my mother's fears. Everything was about keeping my mom's fears at bay. Everything. So when kids in my class with whom I laughed and shared answers for tests started seeming like they could become friends, they naturally asked me over to play or go on trips to McDonald's with their families. Pretending to myself that it might happen this time, my mother might let me go, I paused for a beat, gulped, then said, "Sure . . . " When I reached home and asked to go, my mother sobbed and yelled. Within five minutes, she shouted at me, "Don't you know? Don't you know I feel horrible that I can't let you go? I want to let you be a normal kid. Why are you making me suffer like this? Why are you asking for something impossible? Are you just trying to make me look bad?" I slunk to my room and cried. And the next day, I said to my new friend—who was no longer my friend within a couple of weeks—the day I was supposed to play with her, "I'm so sorry. I can't come over today." When she asked why, I lowered my eyes so I wouldn't have to see the words leaving my mouth. "Um, my grandma died last night. I have to be home with my mom."

It was always my mother's suggestion. "Look, just tell them your grandmother died. Nobody will blame you for that. And stop asking. I can't do it yet. Give me time."

So I killed her, the woman who gave birth to my mother, the woman who made her the way she is. I killed her, over and over again, pretending that it was an unexpected tragedy that meant I couldn't come out to play or go on a field trip or be part of a sleepover birthday party. My mother told me to kill her.

She taught me how to pretend.

• • •

When I was about seven, my mother started experiencing panic attacks. I don't actually remember any of her panic attacks. I've been told that those first few were so strong that she was forced to structure our entire lives to avoid them.

I do remember when our lives started shutting down. After my mother found out my father had cheated on her, she stayed with him. But she intended to make him pay. They fought, every day, every single day. She grew scared as soon as my father left her sight. She started fixating on dogs and cats and unfamiliar situations, then anything that required us to leave our homes. She was constantly, loudly terrified that my brother and I would be hurt or killed if we ventured into the world.

My father once told me that she kept him awake, late at night, all night, demanding that he tell her, "How do I know that's really our kids? How do I know they haven't been replaced by robots?"

I was too young to understand any of this, my brother three years younger. I had never heard phrases like OCD or panic disorder or borderline personality disorder. Years later,

I read about these, then about narcissism, and I experienced the recognition of having a name for how I had been raised. But that was long, long, long after I endured the darkness of that house.

My mother kept us safe by keeping us in the house. Our world grew smaller by the year. My brother and I could play in the backyard by ourselves, but only for a few minutes when she was doing the dishes, so she could watch us out the kitchen window. We were not allowed in the front yard by ourselves: too much openness. There could be a drive-by shooting, a kidnapping. Or we might try to run away, the way I did once when I was ten, attempting a getaway on my skateboard down the alley across the street. I put on my knee and elbow pads first. I didn't make it far.

We went to school. But we couldn't do plays or anything that required time outside of school where my mother could not be in the room. Sports were fine, because she and my father could sit in the car off the field and watch us play catch with our team. They were the most loyal fans. But field trips without them? Never happened.

I was not allowed to visit a friend's house, by myself, until I was seventeen. And that one-hour trip to my friend Sharon's house required three months of negotiating.

Anything outside of the structure, the expected, the rules of the house? Not allowed. It terrified my mother. And her fear always came first.

What I was not allowed to do:

- Have friends, unless they were willing to come to my house every day.

- Cultivate hobbies, other than reading, because those would mean leaving the house.

- Walk down the street by myself, looking in shop windows.

- Ride my bike down the block and around the corner for a few moments, until I was sixteen.

- Get my driver's license, until I was twenty-one.

- Have my own opinions, since those were dangerous weapons against the shell of pretending in our home.

- Be angry.

- Ask any questions at all.

My mother had questions. Thousands of questions. Besides keeping our lives entirely restricted, the other way she staved off her panic was to ask us Questions every night, just after dinner, when the dishes were cleared. My brother, my dad, and I sat at the little table in the kitchen nook, surrounded by the black-and-white line drawings of a city—I always imagined it as New York—on the contact paper my mother had pasted to the walls. On the nights that Questions lasted for longer than fifteen minutes, I stared at those buildings, the empty windows, wondering about the lives that might be inside, willing myself in there instead.

She stood in front of us, took a breath, looked at the ceiling, and began.

"Did you get near any dogs today? Did any dogs get near you? Were you scratched by a cat today? Did a cat scratch you? Did any dogs or cats hurt you today? Were you hurt by any dogs or cats today? Did you leave school today? Did anyone take you from school today? Did a dog bite you today? Were you bitten by any dogs today? Did you run away today? Did anyone invite you to run away today? Were you kidnapped today? Did anyone kidnap you away from school today? Did anyone hurt you today? Were you hurt by anyone today? Do you swear your answers are true? You're not lying? Are you telling the truth? Do you promise you are telling the truth?"

It was the same questions every night, asked the same way every day. She interrogated us, in active and passive voice, every evening. Sometimes she paused for a long time between questions, perhaps to interrogate her own mind, to search the corners of every memory of when she had been afraid that day to feel if any cobweb of fear remained. Fear always remained. In later years, when our verbal assurances were not enough to assuage her fear, she had us sign little slips of paper saying, "I swear I have told the truth today." We each signed and dated those slips. In the kitchen was a drawer with hundreds and hundreds of those slips of paper, bunched up, folded, and curling in on themselves.

Questions started when I was seven and happened every night until I turned seventeen.

Within a few months of this terrifying ritual beginning, I realized it was not going away. The best nights, it lasted fifteen minutes or so. Those were the nights when we looked down at our laps, made our voices small, and did as she asked.

Were we kidnapped and then magically returned to school before the end of the day?

No. Of course not.

Did we get near dogs?

No, never. Of course not.

So we learned to lie, early on. We said what she wanted, night after night, so it would end. *Did anyone hurt us?* Every single night I wanted to look up at her and say, "You are. Right now."

And my dad, who sat there passive, what did he do? Most nights, he willed himself to shut down and get through it. I begged him, in a loud whisper behind his back as we walked into the kitchen, to please not make a fuss, please go along with it. Maybe we could play Monopoly when it was done and go back to pretending that it had never happened. Most nights, he did. We signed our lies on a slip of paper, then stalked away from each other, silent.

But some nights, at least once or twice a week, he exploded. He stood up and shouted at her that this was deplorable, it had to end, she was crazy. CRAZY. Mostly, though, he wanted to fuck with the rules. We were required to stay in the kitchen. So he stood in the doorway, dancing his foot over the line between the kitchen and the living room. If he stepped over the line and put his foot on the living room carpet, she let out a terrifying angry scream. He ran into the other room. She chased him. My brother and I huddled in the nook, him snuggling against my knees. If it lasted too long, however, I got up and begged them to stop fighting, to stop yelling. "Please. Please. Come back to the kitchen," I cried. My father screamed that he was leaving. He threw clothes into a suitcase as fast as he could and grabbed the keys. My brother and I ran to the other room and grabbed our baseball bats. We stood in front of the door, bats cocked, telling him he couldn't leave us. *Please don't leave us.* He did leave, once or twice. He spent the night in a hotel or in his car. I didn't sleep at all those nights because my mother spent the entire night howling in fear. I stayed near her, trying to console her, trying to convince her to stop screaming. Most nights, however, my father stayed. On the nights my father erupted into a fight with my mother—about once a week—and they kept us up for two or three hours of fighting, he finally gave up. He would slump back into the kitchen nook at midnight, all of us in a row, wiping away tears, ready to start being interrogated again.

And almost every afternoon, after school, when my dad returned home from his teaching job, they fought—giant shouting matches with nasty resentment flung across the room. Dad stomped to the den, my mother to her bedroom. And afternoon after afternoon, I walked over to Dad and tried to talk some sense into him and make him see what she was saying. And he would say, "Well, you tell your mother . . . "

So I would walk to her room and try to talk some sense into her and make her see what he was saying. And she would say, "Well, you tell your father . . . "

I went back and forth until I could coax them out to meet in the middle and shrug into a tense cessation of the screaming. I could breathe again.

My little brother was usually taking a long bath during this. I was his protector too. He didn't need to be part of this. And after so many of these fights, when order had been restored, my mother would look at me and say, "You know, you're the real adult of the family, Shauna."

I was eight when she first said that.

I learned to pretend, early. My parents may have kept us awake with their fighting until midnight, but I sat at my desk at school with my hand raised, answer ready. No one asked why I looked so tired and sad. My father was one of the coaches of my soccer league. My mother was the president of the PTA, always ready to organize a potluck or fundraiser. I once heard a mother whisper to her misbehaving son as she grabbed him roughly by the arm, "Why can't you be more like Shauna? Such a nice family. And she's top of her class." He caught my eye, anger there, and I looked away, embarrassed. I wanted to shout, "You have no idea." Instead, I pretended I didn't hear her and walked away.

When we walked down the street, we had a drill. As soon as one of us spotted a dog about to walk by us, we would call out to Dad to let him know. My brother and I moved behind our mom and my dad stood in front of us, his arms outstretched. And when the dog and owner walked by our side, he sidled to the left of us, arms still out, to be a buffer between us and that beagle. When the coast was clear, we were allowed to walk a few feet apart again. One day, however, no one caught it in time. We were walking from our car to the public library and a dog was suddenly on us. My mother shouted out my father's name, repeatedly, increasingly agitated. He somehow didn't make the buffer in time, so she shoved us into the bushes a few feet away to keep us a safe distance from the dog. That's how all four of us stood up against the ivy-covered brick wall of our library, my father in front of us, arms outstretched, as a chihuahua walked by with her very confused-looking owner. When she passed, we looked down, stepped out of the bushes, and walked into the library to check out books. We didn't talk about it.

We weren't allowed to talk about it.

Around the same time, when I was sixteen, people in Chicago started dying after taking Tylenol. The first two were children. It turned out to be some terrible person, tampering with individual bottles and adding cyanide. Then, the copycats began, in places around the United States. Finally, the drug companies started putting safety seals on all bottles of over-the-counter medication, followed by all packaged food. That assuaged the public's fears but only intensified my mother's anxieties. Every time we opened a new bottle of ibuprofen for cramps or the plastic bag inside of a box of crackers, she called me over and demanded I stand by her to witness the opening. Afterward she would ask, "Was it closed? Was it sealed? It's open now but it was sealed before?"

"Yes, Mom," I would say in a monotone. And then I would go to the record player, put on my headphones, and pretend it hadn't happened.

My sophomore year in college, I was informed that I had to sign up for classes that ended before noon. My brother, a junior in high school, was allowed to push a little harder for freedom because he was a boy. He fought and fought for the chance to do a play production in school. My mother relented. But the only way she could allow him to attend rehearsals, after school was done for the day, was to have me as her safety person. Did his play rehearsals take place in the same building as his classes? Yes. Did it make any sense as to why she needed me there? It never did. Best I could understand, she believed she could not handle the unknown of me at college thirty minutes away when my brother was doing play practice. She thought she couldn't handle worrying about both of us. Since I had been her safety person for a while, she would not let my brother act in a play unless I agreed to her terms. And when I pushed, she cut herself and told me I was being selfish by making her suffer.

So I took a full load of classes at college in the morning, then came home so I could sit in the parking lot of my brother's high school in the afternoon. I sat in the back seat of my parents' car, my father in the driver's seat with the keys in his pocket, my mother next to him, staring forward. I tried to read novels for homework, hunched down in my own depression, underlining relevant passages. But every five minutes or so, my mother would say loudly, "How do I know he's in there? How do I know he's okay?" And I would look up from the line in *Ulysses* I was reading, marking my place with my pen, and say, "Because he is, Mom. He's at rehearsal. He's fine." She asked my father the same question, and then she stopped talking for five minutes, until she started again, over and over, the same question, every five minutes, from three in the afternoon until five. My brother would walk out the front door of his school and slump into the back seat. My mother would sigh with relief, not letting go of all of her air, since it would start again the next day. She amended the after-dinner Questions to include my brother's play rehearsal and my presence in the car. Other than that, we never mentioned this ritual prison. There was no chance of escape. Why talk about it at all?

As I grew older, deeper into my twenties, my brother started making noises about moving out. He had graduated college too. (He had also been required to live at home when he attended college, the same one where my father taught that offered free family tuition.) My brother found a job in our town. He wanted to move to an apartment ten minutes away from home. By this time, the fights were pretty epic, my brother pacing and roaring, like a caged animal screaming out in frustration. I often stayed near him and my mom, trying to calm them both down. I yelled too. There's no question. But I felt so engulfed with guilt for my part in the yelling that I usually quelled it. In the middle of one of these fights, my mother turned to me and said, "Look, your brother is angry with me. Your father is always angry with me. You cannot be angry with me." So I ate dinner instead.

At the apex of one of these fights, my mother disappeared. It wasn't uncommon in the middle of hysterical moments for her to lock herself in the bathroom, threatening to kill herself, then emerge later with a dozen superficial cuts on her arm to show us she meant business. But she always stayed in the house. We had all stomped off to separate rooms, so no one had seen her go. We went outside and called in the darkness. Where was she? We all started to panic. We paced around the rooms, trying to figure out what to do. At one point, an hour later, I made myself an ice-cream sundae, lavished with whipped cream and drowned in fudge sauce, because I needed something to do with my pain and worry. An hour after that, she walked through the front door, bedraggled.

It turns out she had walked out of the house, turned left, and gone into the backyard. She hid in the bamboo thicket behind the house and watched us through the sliding glass doors of our living room, terrified and on the edge of calling the police. When we told her we had been freaking out, she turned to me and said, "Oh, you didn't even miss me. I sat and watched you eat an entire sundae. You were happy to be rid of me."

We went to bed and we never talked about it again.

In a fight later, after my brother had left but I had stayed behind to take care of her, I shouted in her face. And then she snarled at me, and said again, for the three thousandth time, that she was the one who was suffering, and how dare I try to blame her when she just couldn't do anything more. I looked down and started to walk away. And she said, in the nastiest voice I had ever heard her use: "You should have fought me harder. But you don't have the guts."

Ten minutes later, she claimed she had never said it. I was making it up. But I remembered. I filed it away, that snarl, that disdain.

I should have fought harder but I didn't know how. It took me until my late twenties to finally escape and find community, then discover my rage, which is how I finally learned to fight my way free to be real.

When pretending for decades is a survival instinct (and you keep telling yourself there's some hope for normal way off in the distance), it takes a long time to stop pretending.

We never talked about this. There was no family therapy. There were no conversations after the yelling died down. We went back into our shells and got on with it. My brother and I didn't talk about this until we were well into our late twenties, early thirties. He doesn't know I'm writing this book. Neither do my parents. We had one rule in our family: do not talk about this outside the family. We were like the mafia. Never go outside the family.

I'm breaking the big rule here.

It's time to stop pretending.

Enough pretending.

Why am I telling you this story? Because I understand now that this story affected every part of who I am. And I know I'm not alone. My specific story is mine, and when I was a kid, I thought every other family was happy and mine was the only one fractured and broken, alone. I know better now. There are so many of us out there who have suffered in silence and shame.

And it's a complicated story, as every human story has always been. We were loved. I know that. They did the best they could. There were hours in that house filled with soundtracks of musicals, early Charlie Chaplin films on the living room wall through the 16 mm projector my dad brought home from work, and episodes of *I Love Lucy* and Julia Child. My dad taught us to listen to Beethoven's Ninth Symphony and pretend to conduct the orchestra with ball-point pens. My mother arranged picnics at the Hollywood Bowl to make sure we were exposed to great culture. We did science experiments and talked about politics. I have memories of long days boogie boarding the waves at Newport Beach and falling asleep in the car in the dark on the way home. Our home was full of books. My parents helped us with our homework. My dad brought me home the textbook out of which he was teaching poetry to college students to point out that it used "Blackbird" by the Beatles as a poem. I marveled at it, then turned the page to read my first Dylan Thomas poem, then a Carl Sandburg poem, and then I found Emily Dickinson. They played *Free to Be . . . You and Me* on the record player and made tape recordings of my brother and me reading *The Pain and the Great One* back and forth. There were baseball games and family trips and lots of Polaroids of posed moments of happiness. But there were, every day, hours that were dark with dank screaming and nights of no sleeping. I never knew which hour was next. I spent my entire childhood tensed up and listening intently, waiting for the first barking comment that meant we would all descend.

NO SUCH THING AS SAFETY

It's a dangerous business, Frodo, going out
your door. You step onto the road, and if
you don't keep your feet, there's no knowing
where you might be swept off to.

—J. R. R. TOLKIEN, *THE LORD OF THE RINGS*

• • •

I stood on a street corner in Paris, smiling. The sun was
shining. I felt unfettered and alive. There was nobody
calling me up to solve their problems or anyone's feelings
to soothe. And yes, I was singing Joni Mitchell's song in my
head the entire time.

I was in my early thirties, living in London with a
famous person. It was a bit bonkers in that house, but they
were paying me a lot of money to edit a book. So I thought
long and hard about it. Should I set aside all the money
I was earning to pay off my student loans? Or should I
explore London on my own one weekend, taking myself to
a different museum, play, and restaurant every time, then
visit a new European city every other weekend?

Actually, I didn't have to think that hard about it. Feeling unfettered and alive won over my troubled desire for security this time.

That weekend, the first time I went to Paris, I didn't have a plan. This might have been the first time in my life I didn't have a plan. Having been raised by a woman who insisted my father put his arms outward to protect us from dogs walking down the street, my brain automatically made plans, backup plans, and counterplans to every possibility. It exhausted me, all these machinations and spreadsheet-like stretches of detail in my brain, all meant to forestall fear. But a few years before, I had started to release the need for constant safety. So I woke up early on a Saturday, hopped the Tube to St. Pancras train station, and stepped onto the Eurostar. I did not have a hotel reservation in Paris. I spoke only a modicum of French, mostly words for food. It was merely me, on a train, by myself, with a backpack and no plans.

I had never been happier in my life.

I watched the green countryside, hills dotted with white sheep, on the way to the tunnel. I listened to my thoughts. They still wanted to press at the edges of my brain, doubting. But I pushed them back. And then I heard a couple of women speaking in American accents about what to do in Paris. I looked over to see two older women at a table, maps and guidebooks splayed out. I eavesdropped, one of my favorite habits, for a few moments. And then I approached them.

"Excuse me, ladies, I don't want to bother you, but do you think I could borrow a map?"

The older lady looked up at me and handed me a map. *Paris*, it said on the front. Maybe she could see my grin at reading the word. Or maybe she was worried. Something made this woman ask me if this was my first time in Paris.

"Yep!" I said. "And I have no idea where I'm going."

I was exuberant about it. She was probably horrified. Gently, she put her hand on my wrist and pulled me down next to her. "I've been to Paris so many times. Let me share some places with you."

And so she proceeded to write on my map the location of her favorite walk-up hotel, right around the corner from the Jardin des Tuileries. She circled the street corners where I could find the best croissants, the best café au lait, the best place to nurse a glass of wine at night and watch the people walk by on the street outside. She told me to go to the Louvre, so I could see it, but spend more time at the Rodin Museum and the Picasso Museum. She told me about her favorite stationery store, where I could find fountain pens and thick paper with the texture of muslin that would drink up the ink of that pen I needed to splurge on. "Write it all down," she told me. I thanked her and went back to my seat to study the map like a guide to the rest of my life.

I thanked her again when the train glided into Gare du Nord. I walked up the steps of the train station and emerged. The weak February light in Paris was the most beautiful I had ever seen. I stood near the park and breathed in the smell of grass and freedom. I found the hotel—tiny and charming—and booked a room. I strolled through the gardens. And I walked, all afternoon, stopping only to eat crepes at a street stand or pastries in a shop where no one spoke English. I pointed and paid.

Hours later, I stood on the Champs-Élysées. People walked by me quickly, brushing by me, not noticing me at all. No one needed me. No one tried to pull me back from the curb. I was alone. I stepped into a Tabac to buy a phone card, the impulse to call anyone at home, even my parents, so strong that I walked inside without even noticing. Once inside, I turned around. No one needed to hear from me all weekend. Right now, I was gone.

I stepped outside at the precise moment the sun broke from behind the clouds. Sunlight hit my face and warmed me. I closed my eyes and tried to breathe it all in. I was in Paris, by myself. Thirty-three years old and I was finally free.

A few years earlier, I had been sitting on the kitchen floor of my apartment on the rural island where I was a high school teacher, throwing a phone against the wall in rage.

At twenty-nine, I had been living away from my parents' home for only two years. I loved teaching and the confidence I was slowly finding in relationship with other people. But on the nights when I had dinner parties with colleagues in my home, the phone rang by ten at night. I excused myself and went to my bedroom to pick up the phone. "When are they going home?" my mother insisted in a hissing voice.

"Mom, it's Friday night. I'm having a dinner party."

"I know. But I want to go to bed soon. And you know I can't go to bed until you get rid of them."

I hung up the phone and turned down the music as I walked into the room. I smiled at my friends and started to clear the dishes. "I bet we're all tired," I said. "Friday after a long week. I know I am." They picked up the cue. They stood to help with the dishes and grabbed their coats fifteen minutes later. I called my mother and told her that yes, everything was okay.

The day I moved into that apartment I was giddy with excitement. My mother sulked as she made my dad help me move my new couch in. My brother lugged a chair up the stairs. The stereo sat in the corner. Time for them to go.

As they finally turned to leave, my mother sobbed again. For months she had been telling me I was cruel, leaving her when she couldn't handle it. "Couldn't I understand?" I hugged her stiffly, not saying anything. I was learning to not engage. As she started to walk toward the door, she said, "I'll talk to you tonight."

"What?" I said. "There will be nothing new to say. I'll talk to you soon."

And she looked at me with that look—half anger, half pathetic begging—and said, "You have to help me. Just give me a little time. I'll call you at night to say hello to know you're alive. Just a little while."

She called me every night for the next two years, insisting that I kick out my guests because she wouldn't feel at peace until she knew I was in my own home, no one else there, the doors and windows locked, in for the night.

Over those two years, I found real friends, friends with whom I could share this story. They all told me the same thing. I had to disengage from my parents. I had to stop waiting for them to get well. I had to start living my own life. One day, in the faculty room, I saw a pamphlet for the National Endowment for the Humanities' summer grants for teachers. The year before, I had seen a similar pamphlet and homed in on an opportunity made for me: an all-expenses-paid trip to New York to study the poetry of Walt Whitman and Emily Dickinson at Columbia University for a month. But the year before, I thought hard about it and put down the pamphlet. My brain, still hardwired to take care of my mother, said, "She won't be able to handle it." The spring of my twenty-ninth year, I took home the pamphlet and applied that day. A few weeks later, I found out I was one of only a dozen teachers across the country to be accepted. I was giddy. My friends threw me a party. And then I had to tell my parents.

I had never been to a new city by myself, not once in my entire life. The most miserable year of my life happened when I was sixteen, living in London with my family. My father had won a Fulbright teacher exchange with a teacher who lived in south London. So we traded jobs, houses, cars, and lives with a family we only met briefly at a conference in San Francisco. We arrived, ready to live fully in the history and wonderful rush of London. Instead, my mother's phobias tripled in size from being in a strange city halfway around the world. She spent the first two weeks sobbing, begging to go home. My father, somehow, held his ground. So she compensated by refusing to allow my brother and me to go to school. We had to stay in the house, with her, reading books and studying what we could, while my father was gone. And by a few months in, my mother was so terrified all the time that she insisted that we sit in the same room together, a couple of feet away from each other. If my brother had to go to the bathroom, my mom and I shuffled down the hallway with him and stood outside the door waiting for him.

I'd rather not think about that year anymore.

So the idea of being in New York City by myself, just before my thirtieth birthday, was far bigger than the fear of telling my parents I was going.

My mother started sobbing as soon as I mentioned casually that I would be going to New York that summer.

My father, who was always on the line when we talked, but never said a thing, heaved a sigh. My mother went into her usual wind-up, growing more and more scared, then angry, and then furious. I didn't say much. I knew if I started to talk, she could twist my words. So I repeated, "It's done, Mom. I'm going."

And then she wailed at me something I had heard many times before: "You can't do this to me. You're my safety person."

She had been telling me this for years. It's the reason I had to sit in the parking lot with my parents while my brother did play practice, why I had to live with them after I graduated college, why she couldn't let me move out of her home until I left. If I stayed with her, she could ask me questions about her experiences, to confirm that everything had been all right, since she didn't trust her own brain. If I left for NYC, then she would be adrift in the world. I had to let go of this dream to keep her sane.

Something in me snapped. I could feel it in my gut, a raw power driving up from my stomach, up to my throat and out through my arms at the same time. It was rage, my first taste of rage. And it was clear and decisive, without any questions. "FUCK YOU," I shouted at her, then I threw my phone across the room and watched it slam against the wall. I sat there for a moment, feeling the rage in my arms, my fingers, the end of my hair. But mostly, deep in my gut, in my feet on the floor. I walked over to the phone, picked it up, and smashed it on the floor. Her safety person? I don't think so.

In that moment, my brain kept chanting one thing: enough pretending, Shauna. Enough pretending that some-day she's going to get well. Enough pretending that the path to my own life was her permission. Enough pretending she was ever going to kill herself, after more than twenty years of threatening it and never doing it. Enough pretending that curtailing my life and allowing her to call me every night would ever heal her. She was the only one who could decide she wanted to heal. Enough.

Enough.

Enough.

The next day, I bought a new phone. The first call I made was to the telephone company, to ask them to change my phone number. The next call was to my brother, to tell him that I couldn't talk with my parents for two weeks—"Tell them I'm fine. I don't want to talk with them." During that time, I plotted out my trip to New York, went out to dinner with friends and stayed out late, went to Seattle to wander the streets by myself and meet friends to go dancing and come home on the 2:10 a.m. ferry. My god, it all felt good.

By the time I called my mother two weeks later, I was mostly free. She was cold and angry with me, snotty. And then I got off the phone. I told her I'd talk to her the next week. She didn't call me back.

It was the first time I learned that I could set the terms.

And the first time I set foot on a sidewalk in New York City—as I stepped off the M60 bus from LaGuardia through Harlem to Columbia University—the very first second, I knew. *I have to move to this city. This is my home.* So I spent that month in New York giddy and drunk on life, walking down Broadway and staying out all night, kissing a Slovenian professor on the lawn, going to jazz clubs and the *Late Show with David Letterman* and the Statue of Liberty and saluting her from the boat, laughing in a cab on the way to Brooklyn with newfound friends, the wind on my face, grinning.

The clackety-clack of the subway trains on the track, the smell of puddles in summer by the curb, the taste of hot dogs from a cart in Central Park, the cool air of the Temple of Dendur room in the Met, and the sight of all those people swarming by me on the sidewalk, yellow cabs streaking by, and me studying every single face, because every last one of them was beautiful to me. I had never been so alive.

I returned to my rural island and quiet life. Too quiet, suddenly. I still loved teaching. But I needed a fresh start. I started therapy for the first time, with a kind woman who asked me basic questions and nudged me. I enjoyed every one of my friends. I couldn't wait to get back to New York.

My mother insisted that she was going to buy me a gun.

Flying off to New York, almost all of my possessions sold, the rest packed into two suitcases, was the most daring thing I had ever done. My brain had chanted *ENOUGH*, and I knew what I had to do. Don't misunderstand—I was terrified. The inside of my brain sometimes chanted the worst hits of my mother's fears. Sometimes it felt like the plane would crash simply because I had stepped on it. And I could feel her fingers curled around my ankles, trying to drag me back. I stared out at the stars, velvety bright in the dark sky, and knew I was heading to the life I had to live.

(Thank you to Mary Oliver's poem, "The Journey," which I read so many times that year, and so many times on that flight, that its language is woven into the memory of my own journey.)

For months, every night, as I lay on my futon in my new room, I dreamed I was running through wide open spaces: fields, piazzas, elementary-school playgrounds with no one on them. It took months for those dreams to not be nightmares.

I was lonely. I had moved from a loving, close community on my island to knowing no one in all of Manhattan. My dear friend Sharon, with whom I was still best friends, lived in New York. But three days after I arrived, giddy and scared, she left for a month in Oregon with her dad. She gave me her apartment to stay in until the first of the month when my room in the apartment on the Upper West Side would open. And she left me with no one to talk with. I stayed in her apartment all day after she left, only leaving her room for the trip down the street to get takeout from her favorite Chinese place, and sat in front of the television to watch Princess Diana's funeral all day.

Once I had moved into my apartment, nodding hello to my new roommates, I wrote letters to friends and walked the streets, memorizing neighborhoods I had only read about in books. All day long, I exulted. But as soon as it grew darker, my mood dropped. The loneliness of talking to no one but my roommates, who felt removed and formal to me, was like being flayed with a cold, biting wind every night. I never wondered if I had made the right move. I knew it would feel like this. But my god, the loneliness.

My brother gave me a great piece of advice in an email: "Just practice talking to people a few more minutes than you think you can. Just one more minute. Two more minutes. It will get easier that way." I took his advice. In diners, I talked to waitresses and the customers in the booth next to mine. My mind screamed I was being a nuisance, boring, a waste of space. I pushed down that voice and kept talking. A lifetime of loneliness and social awkwardness meant I felt neurotic and not worthy. So I practiced it, the way I learned the cello when I was six: slowly, painfully, making terribly creaky sounds. Eventually, I could play a few notes without wincing.

Within a few weeks, I started my master's in humanities program at NYU. I met a flamboyant Dominican man named Carlos who became my new best friend within a few months. Caroline was a high school teacher, coming down to the city from her home in the Hudson Valley for classes a couple of times a week. I loved being part of class discussions about literature again, even though I quickly realized that this master's program felt sort of useless to me compared to the solid, commonplace wisdom I had found in teaching high school. Sharon returned home and we started hanging out, then she introduced me to her friends. By Christmas, I started to feel all right.

Thanks to a reference from someone at NYU, I found a psychoanalytic center nearby. Highly respected therapists with offices on the Upper East Side worked there one day a week and offered services on a sliding scale. I was assigned a female therapist randomly.

My goodness, bless that random choice.

My therapist sat behind me as I lay on a black leather couch in a darkened room. I couldn't see her face. It drove me crazy that I couldn't see her face. It made me deeply anxious, even though I couldn't name why then. After all, I had spent a lifetime being finely tuned to other people's emotions as soon as they flitted across their faces. I was trained to read my mother's slightest wince so I could jump to take care of her. But my therapist sat behind me, taking notes without saying much. I kept looking for her approbation. I didn't find it in her silence. Instead—and this took me years of working with her to realize—in her silence I could hear my own voice for the first time. In the space where

I couldn't see her face, I looked up and watched my own words bouncing off the ceiling. In that space, I could hear myself for the first time.

She was deeply empathetic. Every session, she said a sentence with such kindness in her voice that I felt she understood. Sometimes, for a moment, I could reach a place where I couldn't hear my mother's voice telling me I was a bad daughter, a bad human being, for being in New York and living my own life. I had never known that someone could be so empathetic without jumping in to fix the problem immediately. She never took the burdens off my shoulders. She showed me I could remove them myself, by making myself vulnerable. Working with her taught me that security can be a prison. Being willing to take chances and not know where I was going? That was the path to happiness.

For more than a year, I rollerbladed the loop around Central Park every day. There was nothing like the swoop-swoop of my body on wheels, my legs working hard, the sun on my skin, and I was in the middle of Manhattan, no cars around, alive and kicking. For a couple of weeks, I bladed in the street to tutoring gigs. (I left NYU after a year but stayed in the city to tutor high school students in SAT and their college application essays, which left me with plenty of free time.) But even with a helmet on, I didn't feel right. I realized that I didn't want to become a daredevil senselessly rebelling against the way I had been locked inside my mother's house. I still had common sense. I returned to the park.

Working with my therapist taught me the beauty of clear boundaries. I had never known them before.

The third year I lived in New York, I left for a few months in London to live with Famous Person. I had waited all my life to move to New York, and then I moved away. The experience called. I didn't know where I was going. So I left.

My therapist—with whom I conducted phone sessions for those five months in London—was proud that it took me only a short while to realize my new employers were an eerie simulacrum of my family. There may have been an original Salvador Dalí painting on the wall outside my room and a personal chef who made all our meals, but that place was cuckoo. Still, the weekend trips to Dublin, Florence, Prague, Amsterdam, and Paris made it all worth it. The day I had breakfast in Prague, lunch in Paris, and dinner in London, I started to think I might be done with this grand adventure. The night Famous Person's partner chased me around the grand piano in the middle of a fight they picked with me, I knew it was time to leave.

It was time to go home to New York.

One of the last weeks I was living in London, I had been invited to the opening of the Tibetan Peace Garden on the grounds of the Imperial War Museum. For years, I had been interested in Buddhism, reading every book I could find. As a kid, when things were hard in my house, the only way I could escape was to train my eyes on a white space on the wall and breathe. So when I found out the Dalai Lama would be there that day, I climbed into the ludicrously long limousine to the event.

There were loud Tibetan horns as the sun shone brightly on the faces of British schoolchildren lining the iron railings of the fence outside the garden. Everything— everything—felt alive and warm and whole and good. I can still remember the cast of light on the blades of grass in front of me as I watched the little yellow umbrella held above the head of the Dalai Lama as he leaned down to

look into the eyes of every child. I still remember the s
of the banks of photographers' cameras clicking awa
the Dalai Lama stood on the stage above them. Mo
though, burned into my brain in awake happiness, is the
sight of the Dalai Lama—the most beautiful man I had
ever seen—scanning the crowd and stopping on my face.
We looked at each other for a full minute. (A minute can
be a really long time.) We smiled at each other. We both
giggled. And then he waved at me. And I waved back.

I don't remember another thing that happened that day.
I don't remember much of what happened in the sad, crazy
house before I left. All I knew was that when I returned to NY,
I would find a Buddhist center and start sitting meditation.

• • •

The first time I sat meditation, in a group, with a gentle
voice leading us through the mechanics—sit still; try
to focus on your breathing; if you catch yourself thinking,
simply say to yourself, "Thinking!" and go back—it took me
only about two minutes to convince myself that I was a total
failure. I couldn't stop thinking. I couldn't find any quiet. I
wanted to squirm on my cushion. *You're such an idiot. Stop
thinking!* About ten minutes later, I noticed that I had found
some spaciousness, a full thirty seconds without my brain
nattering at me. And I thought, *Oh, someday I'm going to teach
this.* I noticed that. I noticed that my brain either shouted at
me for not being good enough or thought I was so good that
I could be an expert. (*Pick me! Pick me! I'm the best meditator there
is!*) I noticed that I did that often.

As I sat meditation, first once a week, then three times a week, in that wonderful center on Twenty-Second Street, up on the seventh floor, I noticed that the voice with which I talked to myself shifted from "You idiot!" to "Hey, you're thinking again," to an almost-laughing at the silliness of my monkey-chattering mind going at it again, to a simple, emotionally neutral "thinking." I sat for longer and longer at home. I walked around the streets of New York, noticing how everything felt blown wide open in my heart after leaving an evening retreat, all of the city so impossibly beautiful. I took on another journey, months of weekend-long meditation retreats called Shambhala Training. I found some of the best friends of my life in people with whom I didn't talk until after the end of the weekend, Sunday evening, over tea. We learned about basic goodness. We learned to raise energy to send compassion to others.

I noticed that I still wished for the "perfect sit" at first, the Zen nirvana I imagined of no thoughts at all. I noticed that I softened when I learned that the perfected ideal that had kept me from practicing Buddhism wasn't possible, and thus not the point. Simply showing up and sitting is enough. I noticed that deep into that training, I had a forty-five-minute sit in which I had two thoughts. I simply existed, surfing the waves of the molecules of the room and listening, simply being. Afterward, I had a conversation with one of the master teachers. I talked about the sit, how amazed I had been, how incredible it was. He looked at me kindly, then quietly said, "Now, go sit again." I noticed that the next sitting session was the loudest my mind had ever been. I noticed that I didn't get up to leave but stuck with it.

I noticed the time I was sitting meditation with the group, looking out the window at the building across the street, and

I heard a loud squeak of a door opening. I noticed th
immediately, angrily, wanted to kill whoever had come in
the room to disrupt the peace. And I noticed how my mind
immediately imagined leaping up from the cushion, going
to the man I had yet to see, and helping to heal his wounds.
I noticed that I both wanted to kill him and heal him. I
noticed that.

One weekend, the theme was compassion. Our teacher
explained that there are two kinds of compassion: true compassion and idiot compassion. "Americans mostly practice
idiot compassion," he explained. "They think they need to
give away all their money and energy and time to be good
people. And then they are spent and exhausted. True compassion means that every time you go into a room, you look
around to see who in the room needs the most compassion.
But you count yourself as one of the people in the room."
This had never occurred to me.

Later in the weekend, it was my turn to sit in front of
the group, to ring the gong, to hold the space and be in
charge of the session. I sat on a cushion, my toes tucked
under my legs, and immediately went somewhere deep. In
that deep state, I could access a reality that was hyperreal:
I saw the floral display with the flowers in bud, in bloom,
and wilting in death, all at the same time. I saw inside the
skulls of my fellow meditators. I could see the air quivering,
the molecules parting around people's heads. (Seriously, I
should never do acid.) And in that open, porous state, wide
awake, I watched the room fade away and saw before me
the front door of the house I had lived in as a kid. I opened
the door and walked into the kitchen, in the middle of one
of the Questions sessions. I saw my mother interrogating us,
my father with his arms crossed, my brother hunched into

himself, and my eight-year-old self with tears in her eyes. I walked over to her side of the kitchen and held out my hand. She looked up at me, took my hand, and stood up. I walked her to the front door, opened it, and ushered her out into the world. I closed the door behind us.

I looked up to see the timer. I rang the gong. It turns out I had been silently crying the entire time. People walked up to me Sunday evening to say how inspired they had been by my courage. My heart had been so open it had never occurred to me to feel awkward or embarrassed. I was simply there. And I had walked myself out of that house.

Meditation taught me how to sit with my own mind and not hate it. Meditation taught me to live in the glimpses of light I saw in life. Meditation is what compelled me to close my eyes on a busy subway car, feeling the sway on the tracks, and imagine what it would be like to be blind, then suddenly opening my eyes to see everyone and everything in that car. I cried every time.

Meditation is what helped me to sit in a diner, across the table from my dear friend Gabe, and look into my cup of tea, struck silent by the sight of the milk slowly swirling into the darkness, making everything lighter. My friend looked at me and said, "Wait, are you stoned?"

"No," I said. "I'm here."

And in one of the sessions I had with my therapist, that last year I lived in New York, I told her about how this experience, and Buddhist thought, was changing me, kindly, softly, irrevocably. She laughed a low chortle, a sound I rarely heard. "Have you not noticed all the Buddha statues in this center?" It turns out she had been leading me to the same place.

I took refuge and officially declared myself a Buddhist. In the ceremony, my teachers explained that taking refuge didn't mean we were finally safe. Instead, taking refuge meant admitting that we are all refugees in this world. There is no safe space. We could be hit by a bus every time we step out the door. There is no grand plan. Terrible things are not excused by believing that someone bigger is in charge. Instead, in taking refuge, we declare that we have found some rest in this path of acquiring more knowledge of how the mind works, of compassion, in letting go.

Seeking security is the desperate desire to know how the story ends. It's satisfying, of course. But it means we are not alive to the electric moment of now. If we are playing out what is supposed to happen, where are we in it? If we don't know, and have the courage to stick with don't-know mind, we discover. We are alive to it. We are alive.

Even though there is no basic security to the world, we can still choose to love it fiercely.

I was given a Buddhist name at that ceremony: *Chime Pema*. It means ever-blossoming lotus flower. Always on the journey. Always growing. Always reinventing myself.

Meditation is also what helped me to realize I was ready to go home to Seattle. I missed the trees, the sky, the island. And after those four years—living in New York is like dog years, so it felt like twenty-eight for all I learned—I was ready to be near my family again, but on my terms this time. My therapist wondered, for several sessions, if I was doing the right thing. Was I giving in and doing what they wanted? But I knew that, as much as I loved New York, I was a West Coast girl. Going home was not what I imagined when I first moved to New York. But it was the next step in the journey.

And I knew, deep in my bones, that the man I would meet and marry was in Seattle.

Years later, when my husband and I were profiled in the *New York Times* for our first cookbook, my therapist emailed me to say, "I'm so happy to see how well you are doing. You were right. And I'm so proud. I knew you would be all right. How much you have grown." I cried for ten minutes, remembering it all. My husband came in and saw me, gave me a hug. "You okay?"

"Oh yes," I said, wiping away the tears. "This is a good cry."

I still think often of that first day in Paris. My life now is far more mundane. Instead of wandering free, wherever I want, I am mostly shuttling kids back and forth to dance classes and soccer, writing in a room, rarely leaving our island. There aren't many unplanned hours in your life when you are the parent of two small children.

But that memory of Paris is always there for me. When my brain feels tired, I close my eyes and stand where I am, pretending that once I was blind. Every time I open my eyes and feel the warmth of sunlight on my face, I am standing on a street corner in Paris, grinning, my entire heart full, fiercely in love with the world.

AFTERNOON DELIGHT

I t's just after noon. The kids are both in school for another couple of hours. The sun floats warm through the upstairs window, onto our bed. We fall onto our bed, giggling, half naked. My husband and I kiss, the three hundred thousandth kiss, at least, since we met. In the back of my head I hear the song from the '70s by the Starland Vocal Band, "Gonna find my baby, gonna hold [him] tight / Gonna grab some after-noon delight / My motto has always been 'When it's right, it's right.' / Why wait until the middle of the cold, dark night?"

I'll spare you any further description. This isn't *Fifty Shades of Grey*. There's no darkness in our afternoons. I'll close the door now. This is our time, for us alone.

• • •

Y ou taste like truffles," Danny told me, when he came up for air after kissing me. We were standing on the end of a pier in Seattle, at sunset.

Our second date had been at a wine tasting, on a rooftop deck overlooking Puget Sound. We meandered through the afternoon, slowly, laughing and talking. And after an hour and a half, and several glasses of wine, just after telling me how much he loved reading my food blog, he leaned over and kissed me. We ran across the street, holding hands, skipping in the sunlight, happy and laughing.

We walked down to one of the piers, with that golden light bouncing off the water, and kissed and kissed and giggled. We looked each other right in the eyes. We talked, a lot, about nothing much at all. And at one point, he reached out his hands, and pulled me into him, and started dancing with me. I was happy to let him lead.

We walked up the Harbor Steps, holding hands, in the moonlight, kissing at every new level. He walked me to my bus, and he held me. He said, once again, breathlessly, "You taste like truffles."

"But I haven't eaten any truffles," I said. "I never have."

"Oh, we'll have to take care of that," he told me. We both grinned. Somehow, we both knew. We were in this, together, for a long time to come.

• • •

I never thought I would meet him. When you're a virgin until you're thirty-five, you doubt there is a person in the world who could love you. I'm not talking about finding someone who loves you the way you deserve. I mean someone who approximates love, who finds you attractive, who holds your hand when you walk down the street. Before I met Danny, I thought that was going to be as good as it got. I never imagined I would find someone who could adore me.

The year before I met him, after finally having sex and shedding myself of that shame, I deliberately took a year off from dating anyone. Finally diagnosed with celiac after all those decades of not knowing what ailed me, I wanted to be alive in my body for myself. And so I bicycled for hours every day, went out on Lake Union with a kayak most days, stayed out late with friends, and cooked every night. I started taking photographs of all those meals, the dinners I made for friends. And I wrote and wrote and wrote. Every night, I threw together a meal, then threw together an essay. Somehow, people started finding my website, *Gluten-Free Girl*. Soon, I had a community. Several times a day I checked my site to find comments from people who had read my stories. Mothers started telling me that my recipes gave them the courage to make food for their kids. It humbled me. It made me want to write more, authentically, telling my truth any way I could. I never wrote about what happened with my family—that was too taboo to consider—but I wrote stories about spilling mushroom stock all over my kitchen floor because I was too invested in figuring out how I would write the triumphant piece about mastering this food and I tripped. I let people know I wasn't perfect. Nothing close to perfect. I was amazed daily by the growing number of names that appeared on my site, all of them lined up, happy to read my writing and meet each other there. This was before social media. This was before a single food blogger had ever received a book deal or a television show. This was before anyone knew what to call a food blog. It was one of the purest, happiest years of my life.

I was returning to a self I had been before my mother's fears tainted everything I thought. I was discovering what it felt like to be in my body without worrying it was not good enough. And my work felt important. I took a year off from dating so I wouldn't be tempted to look.

By the middle of that year, I had already decided that my upcoming fortieth birthday would be my "To hell with the wedding party!" At thirty-nine, I was clearly never going to get married. Inspired by Carrie Bradshaw's decision to tell a friend that she was marrying herself to receive a pair of expensive shoes, I decided to throw a party and marry myself.

Still, something niggled. Was I really ready to shut myself off from the possibility of love? On a trip to New York, I connected with three friends I had known for a decade, all of whom had met their husbands online. If my community of readers was online, then maybe my guy was too? I got my first tattoo in New York, spontaneously: the word YES on my left forearm. There were so many reasons: the last lines of Molly Bloom's soliloquy in *Ulysses*, e. e. cummings poems (I will always be a literature student), the joyful way the word *yes* invites the world in, the way I wrote *yes* and underlined it on my students' papers when they wrote a line or paragraph that astounded me with its clarity.

That yes was a reminder to say yes to the moment as it is, instead of wishing for it to be anything different.

I had thrown fear away and written a book proposal. A literary agent I respected had signed me on its strength. I had said yes to all of it. Why not say yes to opening myself to meeting someone?

And there is this story about John Lennon.

When I was fifteen, and an avid Beatles fan, I read the story of how John met Yoko. A friend brought John to Yoko's odd, conceptual art opening. He walked over to a ladder and climbed it. Hanging down from the ceiling was a magnifying glass. He peered through it, fully expecting it to point to some kind of ridiculousness or protest or anger. Instead, in tiny letters, was the word *yes*. He climbed down the ladder in a happy daze, made his way to her, and they began to talk. They talked all night, ate a bowl of cereal in the morning, and then made love. They were together ever after.

Oh, I want that story, my fifteen-year-old self thought. *Please.*

I never did find that love. For years I didn't meet a lot of men, then I met a lot of men who disappointed me. I was afraid, then bold, then bored. But I did think that if, by some far possibility, that man was out there, the man who would come forward to adore me, he would recognize me by that YES.

I put up a profile on the most popular online dating site, with the following headline: "I'll make roast chicken, garlic mashed potatoes, and flourless chocolate torte. You do the dishes. We'll dance in the kitchen." To my surprise, I was flooded with responses. Write about food and the men come calling. There were cups of coffee and glasses of wine with men who didn't know how to laugh, were not interested in food, or were not ready to date. Every one of them asked me, with a hint of irritation or confusion, "Why do you have the word YES tattooed on your arm?"

The entire process felt the same as the few times I had tried online dating before: strange and untenable. One man even wrote to me, after a volley of interesting emails, upon finding out that I cannot eat gluten: "I'm sorry. You seem great, but I really love bread, and I just can't imagine dating someone who can't eat wheat." Oh god. After six weeks of trying this—and signing with a literary agent—I decided to devote my energies to my writing. Who needed this?

I gave up.

When I told the dating site to not renew my subscription, thank you, they informed me I still had five grace days left. *Who cares?* I thought. *They're all going to be the same.* I vowed to not look at the emails piling up in that account. But curiosity lured me in the day before my subscription ran out. I flicked through all the people who had sent out requests, and even felt a small tug of self-satisfaction that I had made the right choice. *No, no, no, no . . . wait.*

Something in his eyes looked familiar. I clicked on the rest of his profile, and found out he was a professional chef. Damn. Well, now I *had* to answer. But I expected nothing. I sent off a little "wink" back, imagining that I would not hear from him, ready for my dating days to finally be over.

To my surprise, he sent me an email the same day, with only one question: "If a man was to prepare a meal for you, what would you consider the ideal meal?"

That was hard to resist. In spite of my resolve, I sent him this answer: "Honestly, it would be this: one he made with love. With his own hands. In season, beautifully seasoned. Made to connect, every taste an experience, meant to be eaten mindfully. Surprising tastes. Wholly unexpected and familiar at the same time. It would taste of laughter."

He wrote back immediately and we started writing to each other about food, pouring out our favorite tastes and memories from childhood and places to eat. I kept my guard up—after all, I was done, right?—but he kept knocking down my damned guard.

And so I walked into one of my favorite coffee shops, prepared to be disappointed. It was eleven thirty in the morning on a Wednesday, the least date-like time I could imagine. I was writing when he came in. I looked over and saw his eyes. I recognized him. And I still sat there, typing away, as he ordered his coffee. A little abashed at how rude I was being, I walked up to him as he was pouring sugar into his coffee. As I walked from my table to the coffee station, the white sugar flowed downward. Without thinking about it, I smacked him lightly on the arm, and said, "Hey, you want some coffee with your sugar?"

And immediately I thought, *Oh shit, I just touched him. Now he knows I like him. Now I know I like him.*

For some reason, we felt familiar to each other, within the first minute. We talked about food and touched each other's hands and beamed with joy looking into each other's eyes. And we laughed and laughed and laughed. Still, I couldn't believe it would be that easy. I fully expected, when we walked away, that he would wave and say goodbye without asking for my number. He asked for my number. We traded cards. And when he was about to hand me his, the wind came up and blew it down the sidewalk. He chased after it, then gave it back to me. *He chased after that card. He wants me to call him.* And when we said goodbye, he didn't try to kiss me. He leaned in for a hug and he held me. *He held me.* He pressed his body against mine, not in a lascivious way, but in a close way, in an intimate, tender hug. In my head, I kept thinking, *Don't cry, Shauna. Don't cry.* I held him back. And then we parted ways. He told me later that when he was walking back to his apartment, he kept thinking, *What in the hell was that?* And I walked back up the hill, trembling, thinking, *That is the first time anyone has ever truly held me.*

He called me the next day, then I called him back the day after that. That is the last time we went a day without talking to each other. We giggled and kissed on the pier after drinking wine. We had a picnic with food we gathered from little stalls in Pike Place Market. As we were tasting balsamic vinegar, I heard him humming. I couldn't place the song at first, then I realized it was an obscure John Lennon song called "Out the Blue": "Out the blue you came to me / And blew away life's misery." We sat on the little patch of green outside the market and spread out our cheese, Marcona almonds, and salami. Toward the end of the lunch, he said to me, "So tell me about this." He pointed to my tattoo.

I didn't want to tell him. I wanted him to know the story. But I started telling him all the literary references and Buddhist references. I slowed down. And inside my head I said, *Shauna. Quit it. He doesn't have to know the story. You know he's it. You're not fifteen anymore.* So I looked at him and told him, "Well, there's this John Lennon story."

He smiled this impish grin of his. "Oh yeah. You mean the ladder story."

I stared at him for a moment. "Yeah, the ladder story. That one." He nodded and took another bite of his food.

A few days later, he called to say that his paycheck had bounced. The owner of his restaurant was going bankrupt, so the checks were coming back empty. He confessed that he had taken out a payday loan to take me out on our first real date. So he had to cancel seeing me that night. I got off the phone and figured out a plan. I told him to meet me at a whiskey bar downtown. We kissed, then I walked him to a bed-and-breakfast down from Pike Place Market, a little French-type place. When I told him I had booked us a room, he got tears in his eyes. "I wanted to treat you. It's not your fault your boss is going broke. So what do you think?"

And upstairs, when he took off his shirt, I saw that he had a tattoo. On his right arm, he has the word IMAGINE. Below it, a tangerine tree. And in the middle, a rendition of a famous self-portrait by John Lennon. "You have John Lennon on your arm," I kept repeating. "You have John Lennon on your arm."

"And you have Yoko on yours," he laughed, explaining he had the tattoos done in his early twenties. Every girl after had said to him, "Why do you have John Lennon on your arm?"

I understood. And in that moment, I knew that we were getting married.

Come, let this man adore you.

• • •

The first few months Danny and I were together, we couldn't keep our hands off each other. Every morning, we woke up warm in bed together, naked. We rolled over and connected immediately. There was no doubting the depth of our passion. Except, when he returned home from the restaurant at eleven at night, he was more interested in cooking than kissing. He opened a bottle of wine, then heated up potato-leek soup with wild truffle honey, saying that he thought of me when he made it, and then spooned it into my mouth. *Well, that's almost as good as making love,* I would think. We would drink an entire bottle of wine before midnight and fall into bed. Like clockwork, every morning, we made love. Eventually, I relaxed. *He's a morning person,* I thought. *He's tired at night.*

After a few more months of that, I realized I couldn't drink a half bottle of wine a night. I felt sluggish and my brain fogged up. After having been raised by teetotalers, and having been drunk about four times in my life total, I didn't know if Danny was drinking too much. Surely my radar was off. So I let him finish the bottle of wine for me, stopping after one glass myself. Soon after, he brought home six-packs of beer and opened one or two bottles after the bottle of wine. Soon he started waking up later in the morning. Some mornings, he slept in so late we had to drive him to work instead of making love.

Danny didn't drive when I met him. I thought it was a little odd. But he explained that he had always lived in cities, where he could take public transportation. Lord knows chefs don't make much money, so not having to pay for a car, gas, or insurance saved him a lot of money. I liked that spirit. I didn't protest. But after I got pregnant, and my belly started to grow, the responsibility of driving him back and forth grew more and more burdensome. Still, he resisted getting his driver's license.

It was improbable that we got pregnant when I was forty-one. We only tried for about three months, no interventions, no counting days or hormone shots or doing anything beyond the usual fun to make a baby. When I peed on the stick and saw the pink plus sign, I jumped on the bed and woke up Danny. We both screamed with excitement. We had started talking about having children as soon as we moved in together. On one long bus ride to his restaurant, we listed all the things we couldn't wait to teach these imagined children: how to throw a curveball (me), how to make a great omelet (Danny), how to care about other people deeply and not lose themselves (me), how to care about the work that Amnesty International does (Danny). So finding out we would have a child together, a few weeks before I turned forty-two? It was a gift beyond belief.

Everything shifted after I became pregnant. I still loved my husband as fiercely as ever. Aside from my growing concern that he might be drinking too much, I never worried about anything between us. Danny always made sure to wake up early and make coffee, then wake me up with a full cup. He worked harder than any man I had ever met, determined to make great food that would give people joy in their bellies. When he returned home, he put his arms around my belly and turned his head to whisper to our daughter in there. He read her *Winnie-the-Pooh* and poems every day. He rubbed my feet. I made sure he was happy too, asking him about his days, driving him to work, still basing most of our life around making sure his needs were met. And I made him laugh. But I began thinking about this girl's needs more, the girl who flipped in my belly, her head dancing in my pelvis so hard I called her Little Stevie Wonder. I talked with her all day long, felt the weight of her between my hips. The ability of my body to shift and change, to grow a human inside me, began to shift the way I viewed my body. I knew that I would never be the same after she arrived. For years before I met Danny, I wondered if I wanted children. After three decades of being under my mother's thumb, did I want to be beholden to another person? After therapy and all those years of living alone, I knew I did. I couldn't wait to meet this girl.

Danny and I wound our legs around each other in bed and talked about the future. I was so unutterably happy.

So I was shocked down to the bone when Danny started talking, in the darkness of the rides home after work, about his fear that he wouldn't be a good father. "How do I know that I will be okay? How do I know I won't ruin this kid? How do I know I won't hurt her?" I reassured him that he was, without a doubt, the most gentle man I had ever met—fierce and funny and kind. But still, he worried, for reasons I couldn't fathom.

Her birth date approached. Years before, I had a fibroid tumor removed by a doctor who wanted to preserve my uterus. She told me then that if I ever got pregnant, I would have to have a C-section. Fine with me. At least I could have a baby. My obstetrician set a date. In a few weeks, we would meet our daughter.

Danny started to fall apart. He was anxious nearly every day, distracted, erratic. Chefs aren't much good at academics. Danny's brain works in quick spurts and constant movement. I knew this. I fell in love with him. But in those weeks before our daughter was born, it was almost impossible for him to focus. He would start a sentence and I'd watch it trail off in midair. *Is he drunk?* I'd wonder. No, of course not. He's scared. I called his oldest brother and told him what was going on. He remembered feeling the same, so he called Danny to reassure him. Danny's siblings are like gods to him. I thought this would help. It did, for a day or two, but then he started to crumble into nervous energy and terrified pacing again.

Three days before our daughter was due, I drove to Danny's restaurant to meet people for dinner. Several people who were prominent in the food world were in town for a conference. They had reached out to ask if we could meet. Common sense should have told me to stay home, since I was enormous-bellied and barely moving. But a sense this might lead somewhere bigger took over. (*Pick me! Pick me!*) I went in for dinner, late, so I could drive Danny home at the end of the night.

He came to the table to say hello to everyone. I stared at him, mouth open. He was slurring his words so badly he wasn't making any sense. I grabbed his hand and made our excuses, then pushed him toward the door, then outside to the darkened courtyard.

"You're DRUNK!" I shout-whispered. "You're completely plastered. What in the hell?" He started to cry, so I held him and told him to pull it together, since he still had to cook for all the diners. Somehow, working those old pretending muscles, smiling when I was screaming inside, I made it through the dinner and convinced these strangers that Danny was a wreck because the baby was coming and he was so nervous.

He was drunk. Super, sloppy drunk. At the end of the night, I drove us home. He cried, hard, and said, "I have a problem. I think I'm an alcoholic. I can't stop. This is why I'm afraid I'm going to hurt the baby. This is why I don't have a driver's license. I haven't gone a day without drinking since I was twenty-one. Sometimes I drink all day and night. I can't stop. I don't know how to stop."

I stopped at a gas station to fill up the car, but mostly to try to breathe. I stood there in that ghostly neon-green light, pumping gas, thirty-seven weeks pregnant, gasping for air, trying to figure out what to do. My husband was an alcoholic and we were having a baby in three days.

We spent the night crying, holding each other. He wanted to stop, he told me. He just didn't know how to stop. And since we had met, he had been pretending. He was constantly, low-level terrified that I would leave him once I knew the truth. My heart ached for him. I knew the pain of pretending, the muscles it took to keep the lie together in the face of the gaping maw of truth. I wanted to help him, of course. I knew that he had his own lifetime list of reasons he didn't feel good enough. I told him I would be there for him. And I would. But I also knew that the child kicking in my belly, all that night, deserved better than an alcoholic father who could not face his life. When I finally fell asleep, long after Danny passed out, I remembered the part of John and Yoko's love story I glossed over when I was fifteen. For a year, John left Yoko and lived with another woman in Los Angeles. He referred to it afterward as his "lost weekend." And now, here was my guy, the one with John Lennon tattooed on his arm, drunk in the bed beside me.

I knew that I had a hard decision to make.

After I drove Danny to work the next day, I sobbed the entire car ride home. I stumbled into the house, found the couch, and screamed out the pain of it all with a howl. All those years I had been trapped in my parents' house and now I might be trapped in a house with a man I loved who couldn't stop drinking. It took me until my thirties to set up the clear boundaries with my domineering mother. It would not take that long with my alcoholic husband. I called my dear friend Tita, whose father had struggled with alcohol all of his life and never stopped drinking. She listened, then she gave me some counsel. Wise words to use. Clear intentions. The nod that I was doing the right thing to say this had to end.

We wouldn't be able to talk about it for a while. As a surprise for him, I had been saving up airline miles on the sly, so I could fly his sister in for the birth of our child. Still wiping the tears from my eyes, I drove to the airport to pick her up, then drove right to Danny's restaurant. He stood outside, sheepish, waiting to see if I would be mad. When he saw his sister in the passenger seat, he started weeping. We both gave him hugs. He looked at me over her head and mouthed, "Thank you thank you thank you." But in bed that night, when I tried to talk about the future and how he needed to stop drinking, he asked me if we could wait until after the baby was born. "I'm just not ready for my sister to know. I won't drink this weekend, but I can't talk about it with her yet."

So Danny and I spent the weekend pretending that everything was fine. His sister, a woman I adore, had no idea we were dealing with a disruptive crisis. She helped us clean, pack, and prepare. The night before our daughter was born, I asked if we could watch *The Shawshank Redemption*, a movie that had always deeply moved me. Days later, I thought about that movie, realizing that somehow I had known.

The morning our daughter was born, Danny tried to eat breakfast with his sister and me, then ran outside, gagging. He dry-heaved into the grass behind the Buddha statue in our yard in front of which we got married.

And then we were in baby mode. I pushed the reality of his alcoholism into a tiny box in the back of my mind, a compartmentalizing skill I learned early in life. At the hospital waited my brother, his wife, our nephew, my parents, and our dear friend Tita. Danny's sister joined them when Danny and I walked arm in arm toward the OR. Forty minutes later, at 4:40 p.m., with the Beatles singing "I Will," Lucy emerged, with her barbaric yawp of aliveness. Danny cut the umbilical cord and cried. We both cried as they put her on my chest and we watched her eyes dance from him as he talked, then to me as I talked with her. Lucy, bringer of light.

Twelve hours later, precisely, at 4:40 in the morning, I woke with a sudden start in my hospital bed, my legs held by the compression cuffs to prevent blood clots. Immediately, I looked over to the plastic Isolette to my left. Lucy was wide awake, her eyes open, looking at me. I felt flooded with love and cooed to her, talked with her about how happy we were she was here. She looked at me. And then I watched a wave of dusky color go across her face. I jolted. That didn't seem right. I called out to Danny to wake up and call the nurse. When the nurse came in, Lucy seemed fine, the same pink color as before. After checking her, the nurse moved the Isolette aside to check my vitals. I looked over to see the dusky wave again and said, "That! She's doing that." The nurse dropped her stethoscope to her chest and rushed over to the Isolette. As fast as she could, she ran our daughter out of the room. I looked at Danny, frozen. A moment later, we heard "Code blue. Code blue." And I heard the pounding of feet running down the hallway in the direction of where she had taken our daughter. "Danny, go! Go!" I was pinned to the bed, terrified, not able to move. He came back, his face ashen. "All I saw were doctors and nurses huddled. A nurse motioned me back here. I don't know."

We held each other, too scared to even cry.

It felt like an hour before anyone came to talk with us. It must have been three minutes. A doctor told us that Lucy had stopped breathing. They had moved her to the neonatal intensive care unit (NICU), where they would be monitoring her closely. He mentioned something about the prominence of her forehead, which had struck me as enormous when I first saw her. But he left without explaining anything more.

And we couldn't see her until the NICU opened at six.

Danny started crying. I called the nurse in. When she came in, I said, "Get these things off my legs. I'm going to need to be able to walk soon. Let's start now." She was startled but she listened to me. Gingerly, with terrified fury, I put my feet on the floor. And I took a few steps to the bathroom and back. I needed to be ready.

When we finally saw Lucy, she was covered in one of those thin aluminum blankets they give to marathon runners at the end of the race. My mind latched onto that image. We talked to her, stroked her forehead, and heard for the first time the incessant beeping of the monitor measuring her heart rate, oxygen intake, and blood pressure. I can still hear the beep of those machines in my dreams now. Luckily, we also noticed that she was by far the biggest baby in the NICU. In fact, within a few hours, they moved her to the pediatric intensive care unit (PICU) instead, where she had her own room. We stood on either side of her Isolette, willing her to breathe.

On that second day of her life, the doctors put her into an MRI to find out if something unusual was happening in her brain. I sat in a wheelchair just outside the room, looking through plexiglass, Danny holding my hand, as we watched them slowly push her into the huge tube. Within a moment, the technician ran to the MRI to pull her out. She had stopped breathing in there. A doctor ran by us and grabbed her. We rushed back to her room, where they had inserted a breathing tube into her trachea.

I have required sedation every time I have needed an MRI since.

These were the most terrifying moments of my life. And we had no answers for days and days. Friends gathered around with food, brief visits, talks, calls, texts, and hugs.

My parents came to sit with us in Lucy's room once, but my mother's fears made her shriek in terror when one of the little caps someone had knitted fell off the bed onto the floor. She commanded my father to grab it and stuff it in the trash, since it was now covered in germs and would kill our child. I asked them to leave. I didn't have energy for this.

And in the midst of this time, Danny and I were together, without a doubt. We held hands as we stood next to Lucy, holding her tiny hands when the nurse took another round of blood from her, once from her forehead. By this point, she had a breathing tube and feeding tube, into which I would push my meager supply of breast milk from a syringe every hour or two. After the second night of sleeping in our hospital room, I had to be released as a patient. (My kind nurse waited until I was ready to leave to say that she was a big fan of our work.) We slept together on a twin-sized cot in Lucy's room. Danny's drinking was still in that tiny compartment in the back of my mind.

On day three, the nurses urged us to leave for a bit, go outside, get lunch. We had been huddled over her for days. She seemed to have stabilized. Danny and I walked, holding hands, to a taco place nearby. He reached for a beer. And I started to say no, of course, but then I stopped. *Maybe if he just drank when he was with me?* He drank his beer and we ate in silence.

After days of watching our daughter's breathing rate rise and fall, I demanded that one of the nurses take her out of her Isolette. On her second day alive, she had somehow reached up with her newborn hand and ripped out her own breathing tube. She had been flat on her back, hands kept to the bed with little white cuffs, since then. I remembered how much she loved to move inside of me. And of course, she had known my body for nine months. So I sat in a rocking chair and insisted the staff unstrap her and nestle her against my body, wrapping a blanket around her so she could be snug. Within ten minutes, her breathing regulated. Danny and I took turns holding her this way for twenty-four hours. The next day, on Danny's birthday, the doctors took out her breathing tube. They also explained that she had a condition called craniosynostosis, which meant all the soft spots on the front half of her skull had fused before she was born. The condition can sometimes cause upper airway obstruction, which is why she stopped breathing. The day after that, we were moved to a regular hospital room. The next week, we went home, terrified and relieved. We had a long medical road ahead of us, but at least we were home.

Three days later, Danny had to return to work. We talked, right before he left, about not drinking. He pledged to do it. I told him that I knew that alcoholism is a disease. He's not to blame for it. And I would stick with him for a long time. But there would come a time, someday, if he kept drinking, that we would be up against the boundary. And I would take our daughter and move out. He pledged to stop drinking.

At the end of the day, I took our daughter from her crib, buckled her into her car seat, and drove us the twenty minutes to Danny's restaurant. She screamed the entire time. I arrived in a cold sweat. Danny felt terrible. And there was nothing else for us to do. He still couldn't get a driver's license, until we knew he wouldn't drink. He said he had not drank anything that day. I told him I was proud.

Night after night, I buckled Lucy into her car seat. A few days in, I popped in a CD of ocean noises, which was meant to sound like the womb. I blasted it so loud it almost hurt my ears. She didn't cry. I did. I cried every night on the way to the restaurant, with the sound of waves covering my sobs. She slept. I wondered what to do. And every night, Danny swore he had not taken a drink.

One night, he came to the car drunk, about halfway through the second week of work. He slurred his words and lurched at me for a hug. I buckled him into his seat and drove us home, the sounds of the ocean covering my sobs, both he and Lucy asleep. I put her back in bed, then moved him from the car to the couch. I closed the bedroom door and did all of Lucy's feedings in the middle of the night by myself.

This went on for weeks. We would start a new calendar— Day one! Great job!—and then a few days later, he would stumble out of the restaurant. Danny still didn't want to tell anyone in his family about it. Or mine. When he was at work, I called Tita for advice and every time she said, "You will have to decide when you have had enough."

And every day I loved our child more, with a fierce deep compassion. The love I felt for her made me feel connected to every mother in the world, including my own, and to every person who was once a child. So, in essence, every human being on the planet. My heart split wide open when I held her. I felt terrified and sad and protective and still stretching into the unknown without needing to know the answer. But these were, without a doubt, the rawest moments of my life.

I couldn't write about any of this on our food blog. It was too real. And Danny wanted me to keep it to ourselves. And so I lived in a daze, sometimes sobbing, mostly rocking Lucy as I walked back and forth with her from the kitchen to the bedroom while Danny was at work. At the same time, I felt the responsibility to develop recipes for gluten-free clafouti and granola bars and fried green tomatoes coated in grits with melted cheese on top. In some ways, it was comforting to return to work in the tiny moments between taking care of our daughter. But in many ways, it felt like pretending. It set off something in me that felt old and dank, a familiar path I was forced to follow. *Make them hungry. Show them how strong you are! A newborn and you're the one offering new recipes for the masses. You can't talk about your life. Keep it private.*

Gluten-Free Girl had been my private space, the place to write, a joyful glimpse of authentic living. But as soon as we retreated into recipes, not sharing that I was enduring the most terrifying days of my life, I became that kid again who was forced to pretend.

Seven weeks after Lucy was born, I picked Danny up from the restaurant and he was drunk again. On the calendar, we had marked off two weeks without drinking. That was smashed to pieces again. He sat on the couch, holding the baby, and trying to eat the nachos I had made him for dinner. He was so sloppy drunk that bits of olives and jalapeños kept falling off the chips and nearly landing in Lucy's mouth. I grabbed her and put her in her crib. I stood at the door, my hand on the knob, breathing, because I knew what I was about to do.

I found Danny in the kitchen, wiping off his plate. He seemed to have sobered up some. We stood in front of the stove, together, and I told him, in clear, declarative language, that I was done. "Remember that I told you there would come a day we would hit the boundary? Here it is. You're done." I told him he had to call every member of his family the next day and tell them what was happening. I would too. We needed help. He needed to start going to AA meetings.

And if he could not choose his new family over cheap white wine and bad beer, if he would not fight for us by getting better, then I would have to leave.

I meant it too. Enough pretending. Enough.

• • •

He did call his family and mine the next day. He went to an AA meeting every day for three months after. And then he quit his job at the restaurant—a wine bar (!!)—and stayed home with me and Lucy to write our first cookbook. He chose his health and our well-being over his disease.

My parents never did that. Danny did.

We had to wait until Lucy was three months old to find out that the genetic syndrome that caused her craniosynostosis was one of the few that did not cause profound developmental disabilities or death by three. That's when I finally started to breathe. Our daughter endured a nine-hour surgery when she was nine months old. The surgeons removed her skull, rebuilt it, and put it back on her head. Without doing that, there was no room for her brain to grow. Danny and I held hands in the waiting room. He was sober and the two of us somehow managed to laugh over ridiculous websites. She didn't sleep for longer than an hour for four months straight after that. She never really sleeps well, even today. Danny and I kept joking that if there weren't a child involved, surely someone would have called Amnesty International on our behalf.

I had a breast cancer scare when she was eighteen months old. While it wasn't cancer yet, one of my breasts had enough clusters of precancerous cells that my breast surgeon took out a clump of them in surgery. Afterward, I chose to go on Tamoxifen instead of getting a mastectomy, even though I was at very high risk. That caused me to go into early perimenopause and meant we couldn't get pregnant again.

We started the adoption process, which drained our bank account (my parents helped chip in for the second kid, which felt weird, but we're grateful now that he's here). We worked for three years to find him, a long and sometimes dispiriting process. But we kept going. When Lucy was five, Desmond's birth mother chose us to be his family when she was seven months pregnant. We were there at his birth. His birth mother, an incredible woman, wanted me to be the first person to hold him. When they put him in my arms, I felt an enormous love for him. I could feel that he was an old soul, someone who had been here many times before. I also checked his skull immediately. Yep, all the soft spots open and normal.

Suddenly, we had two kids and not enough income, so we did a Kickstarter to launch a gluten-free flour business. Then we had a business that really wasn't sustainable and not even what we wanted, even though we couldn't admit that for a while. And then I had my ministroke. And Danny's folks were growing older, so they had to be helped into assisted living.

You know. Life.

Through it all, we kept writing recipes and presenting cheerful stories about our lives to sell the cookbooks we were creating. And then, we reached the place where we could no longer pretend. Frankly, the election of 2016 was the final catalyst. We quit writing *Gluten-Free Girl*. We stopped living as public personas. We stopped trying to make a living out of our lives. I could no longer make a living at telling half truths.

We have been through all of this together, and it has made us who we are. We're here.

•••

Danny has not taken a drink of alcohol in a decade. When Lucy was nearly six months old, he finally got his driver's license. We felt like equal partners, at last. Every day, I tell him that I am proud. And it's time for the very sexiest thing I can imagine: we're best friends who never pretend anymore. We are for each other. This time together, urgent and laughing, giving each other pleasure, is the best conversation we have. Every day, we are more connected. Every day, we are more ourselves with each other. I hope I have another forty years with this tenderhearted love of mine. I cannot wait to laugh with him all those years from now, when we know each other even more deeply.

FOLLOW YOUR BLISS, MY ASS

Danny and I sat in our car on the ferry, our toddler daughter asleep in her car seat behind us. It was our day off together, nothing holding us down.

We looked at the minivan parked in front of us, its back door open. Inside, a woman moved about frantically. Her hands fluttered from the piles of boxes jammed in the back to a clipboard perched on top. In a panicked motion she patted down the hair behind her ear. I stared for a moment, puzzled, then realized she was looking for a pen. She looked up at me and I held her gaze. She clambered out of the minivan and came to our car. Danny rolled down the window and she asked us, "You wouldn't have a Sharpie on you, by any chance, would you?"

I opened the glove compartment and reached for a black Sharpie. I always seemed to have them in the car for book signings.

"Here you go," I said. "Of course."

She looked near tears in gratitude. "Thank you. You've saved me, for the moment."

We asked what she was doing. She explained that she ran a small business, making and bottling medicinal tea with THC, which she then drove around to every store in the Seattle area that stocked it. She was on a delivery and her printer had run out of ink. So she had to handwrite the company information on the last few boxes. And she couldn't find a pen.

We both told her, at the same time, "Oh, keep ours! We don't need it." She waved and smiled and returned to her box-stuffed minivan to write labels as quickly as she could until the ferry docked.

Afterward, Danny and I looked at each other and said, "Promise me we'll never do that."

• • •

Five years later, Danny was buckling squirmy toddler Desmond into his car seat and asking Lucy once again to stop doing pirouettes and get into the car. I was running the heater in our other battered car before driving to the post office again. I paused before I closed the trunk.

"Hey honey, look at this," I told him.

He glanced over at the trunk full of boxes, some of them with handwritten labels because our printer had broken again. And we both grimaced.

"Remember the lady on the ferry?" I told him.

"Yep," he said.

"Yep," I said.

We gave each other a kiss and drove off.

I never intended to start a gluten-free flour business. You know those kids who always seem to have a hustle, the ones who run lemonade stands, then sell t-shirts, then start creating their own apps when they're twelve? That was not me. Hell, I didn't even know how to balance my checkbook when we started our business. Neither Danny nor I dreamed of being entrepreneurs. My husband is happiest in a restaurant kitchen—since his ADHD brain works best in fifteen-minute bursts—and all I wanted to be was a writer since I was old enough to hold a pen.

So why the hell did we start a gluten-free flour business with an eight-year-old who needed another skull surgery and a six-month-old adopted baby? Not to mention a cookbook in copyedits, due to be published in six months? Were we absolutely insane?

Yes.

And we were broke. Or, perpetually on the edge of going broke, it seemed. Always, always, in the back of our minds was the feeling that we were going to fall off that cliff.

This might surprise you: very few people make real money writing cookbooks. If you're lucky, you get a decent advance. Say $50,000. *That's a lot of money!* Except you only get half of it up front and you have to immediately set aside another 25 percent for taxes. (If you don't, because you need that money to live on, then you'll literally pay for it later.) So that's $18,750. *Still a chunk of change.* But now remember that every single ingredient you buy to test those 120 recipes, over and over again, has to come out of that money. Unless you can make the remaining $8,000 last for the next two years, you're going to need to get another job. So you and your husband take on catering gigs, ghostwriting jobs, and web sponsor-ships for gluten-free food products you love, then gluten-free food products you like okay, then gluten-free food products you write about and promote quickly then walk away because you had no other choice: you had to pay the bills.

Meanwhile you have to keep your website up and running to keep the fans interested until your book comes out. You have to create new gluten-free cookies and write content that gives people hope. You have to post recipes on Twitter, Facebook, and Instagram, and keep responding to the com-ments so that everyone feels heard. Some people are posting shitty comments—knowing you won't publish them—about how gross and fat you are, how ugly your children are, how dumb your husband is, how you're an asshole, how you think you're better than everyone around you. You have to close your eyes before you sit down to the computer and take a deep breath before seeing how few words you can read before you understand it is one of those ones and hit delete right away. You have to schedule time for that every day, because there will be at least fifteen on the website alone, plus twenty-five or more on social media.

Don't forget that you also have two children who deserve your full attention. When you look around at your house, you'll see the dishes piled up in the sink, the baby still not sleeping, the older kid cranky because she didn't want to eat quinoa salad for dinner. You know that when the kids are asleep, you will sit down at the computer again to type up three more recipes and finish a blog post before you fall into bed at midnight. Just after three in the morning, you will wake up with a start from nightmares about the bank account, then go out to the living room and try to read yourself to sleep on the couch.

That's fun.

"You need a side gig," people told us. "Mailbox money. Something consistent coming in." A solid business, something less evanescent than blog posts and comments. We had a huge fan base, people faithfully reading our website for almost a decade. We had a gluten-free flour blend I had created for our cookbooks. No matter how many times I published the recipe or made videos showing people how to make it, readers asked: "When can I buy your flour?" It felt as though people were lining up to give us money.

Every month, we had to hustle to make ends meet. Wouldn't a little flour money help? At first, we imagined blending it ourselves, renting a small commercial kitchen in the town where we live, bagging it up, and putting it in boxes for customers. Some friends urged us to think bigger. "DREAM BIG!" they all said.

Sure, we didn't know what we were doing. But after I started writing my food blog, everything else had arrived as a surprise. The James Beard Award! A feature in the *New York Times*! Teaching gluten-free cooking in a villa in Tuscany! A spot on the Food Network! We had nowhere to go but bigger.

In American culture, the entrepreneur is king. Work hard enough and you too can have fortune, fame, and a private jet. Every example we read seemed to tell us that this is how you do it: work your heart out for five years, then sell to a bigger company and reap your rewards with a heap of cash and time to do what you really want after you have been successful. Shoot for the stars. *Life is short. Follow your bliss.* If our food blog had a well-known name, and pieces about food-industry trends insisted that gluten-free was "hot!" why were we not moving on this? So we started planning.

...

No one tells you just how hard it is to start a small business. It's beautiful, exhausting work. It's harder when you think that you're the only one struggling to figure it all out, to make ends meet, to untangle the knots of a thousand different threads all jammed together in your head. It's harder still when you have to pretend that it's all going fine, no problems here, look how happy we are!

With the help of a friend who believed in our work, we dove into the idea of creating our own company. Thus began the next phase of my life: continually researching things I did not understand. Google would become my best friend.

Best gluten-free co-packers in the Pacific Northwest. Printers for food products. How much more expensive is recycled cardboard than new? How much do graphic designers charge? How to negotiate a deal with a co-packer. Best color scheme for food packaging. How much money do food companies make a year? How do you make money with a food product? Secrets of a successful crowdfunding campaign.

Over the course of a couple of months, while Danny developed cookbook recipes, my friend Claire and I hashed out the details of our gluten-free flour. I would pick up the baby and walk him around after a nap, or put him in the carrier on me and walk as we talked. I would often stop to check in with Danny about a recipe, then walk back to the table to make a decision about a font, a color, or a supplier. For weeks I lived on adrenaline. Those pretending muscles I learned as a child pushed me forward. We were ready to launch.

We launched a Kickstarter in October 2014, looking for funding to make ten thousand boxes of our all-purpose, gluten-free flour blend. Honestly now, simply typing those last few words gives my fingers the jitters. I must have typed them ten thousand times in two years. This was one of the most stressful periods of my life (only slightly less stressful than the seven weeks after Lucy's birth when I didn't know if Danny would stop drinking).

But we made it. We raised $92,000 in four weeks. People believed in us. The media picked up on it. Our little guy crawled for the first time after we came back from the dinner celebrating it finally being done.

And then the real work began.

• • •

The friend who had helped us with the Kickstarter and launching the business left. The first month we were officially a gluten-free flour business, we were hit with a three-week-long siege of flu in our family. From bed, between bouts of vomiting, I researched everything new coming at me. *How to set up a business bank account. How to choose a bookkeeper. Should I run a business without an accountant? How to register for a trademark. How much do trademark lawyers cost? What is the best shipping software for a small business? Which offers the best rates for small business—FedEx, UPS, or USPS? How do I know what size box I need to ship two twenty-ounce rectangular boxes?*

We had cleaned out the garage and set up a shipping station—a table with labels, tape dispensers, blank label pages, and a whole lot of hope. The man who owned the trucking company on our island used his dolly to load it all in: ten thousand boxes of flour, shrink-wrapped, on seven pallets. We stared at all those boxes of flour. In my head, my brain was screaming: *My god, what have we done? I don't know what the hell I am doing here.* But I didn't say it out loud. We had boxes to pack. I puffed myself up with forced cheerfulness and coffee and started packing.

No one tells you this before you crowdfund a project: after your thing is made, you will spend most of your money sending prizes to people who supported you. There were hundreds of boxes of flour to send out as a thank-you, along with gift baskets filled with our cookbooks, flour, recipes, and gluten-free foods. We held a pie party at our cooking studio. We baked and delivered ten gluten-free pies to people in Seattle. There were the five separate dinner parties we had to cook for people who had supported us with substantial pledges. There were promised boxes of flour with the first copies of our new cookbook when it was published. There were pledges for homemade biscotti. Oh, those fucking biscotti haunted me.

We found it impossible to keep up with all the prizes while we were researching how to run a business, while we were packing boxes, while we were raising children, while we were finishing final edits for our cookbook, while we were working three jobs on the side since we weren't making any money from this business yet. We put all the prizes on a schedule, splayed out for the next year, and did our best to keep up.

But every night, I woke up worried about them. For the girl who had only found validation at being the best at everything academic, I was now the woman who was falling behind, not good at something. Flat-out failing.

Two other friends volunteered to help us for free. We didn't have any money—we had less and less money each month—but we promised our friends part of the profits, when we did our second run. We tried to put all the profits from the first round of flour sales into the business savings account for the second run, bigger this time, and not stored in our garage, but with a distributor, who could put it into grocery stores. Brokers had been reaching out to us. A bread company in Seattle wanted to develop a bread with our recipe and put our name on it. There was so much promise ahead. Everyone—everyone—told us the same thing: put in five years of hard work and your bliss will come.

Wake up in the middle of the night, terrified.

• • •

I t wasn't all hard. Emails poured into my inbox, notes of gratitude from people who had been making pies for husbands, cakes for children, and holiday treats that pleased everyone in their lives. We kept going because this flour had become a part of people's families. We felt like we had to keep going for them.

We listened to people's complaints about the cost of shipping—to receive two boxes of flour cost nearly seven dollars in postage—so we began talking about rebranding. If we put the flour into four-pound bags, people could buy more. And then we could get the flour onto the biggest online shopping site, which meant free shipping for customers. *Should we look for someone to co-brand this with, a company that would want to produce the flour, absorb the costs, and put our name on it for a licensing fee?* One of our friends helping in the business said we should really think about getting three or four more licensing deals, since that is where all the money was, not in flour. Build the name, then start selling the name.

How much does a licensing deal pay? What companies started in someone's garage and became a big success? Cost of reprinting new labels. Cost of heat sealer for bags. Cost of recycled bags with plastic windowpane. How much cut of sales will the online site take?

After one of these meetings, my head spinning, I looked out the window of our cooking studio. It was on a farm on our island. Outside, sheep chewed on the grass, slowly, going nowhere. I envied them. If only life were that easy. I came back to the avalanche of details I had to decide on and sighed. It floated up into my mind, this thought. *I guess I'm not a writer anymore.* There was no time. There would be no days of sitting in front of the computer, trying to make sense of the world through the sentences I created. I had gluten-free flour to sell.

Three days later, I was sitting in one of those meetings when I started losing sensation on the left side of my body. My transient ischemic attack shook me to the core. My doctor informed me that 20 percent of people who survive a TIA have a full stroke within the first three months. I had to rest.

Still, our next cookbook would be published two months later. Even though I was exhausted and recovering, we had to come up with a plan. Publishers, even the best of them, don't do much anymore to promote individual books. They publish so many that they expect those of us with social media followings to promote them ourselves. I took a deep breath and dove in. *Pick me! Pick me! Pick my book to buy this fall!*

The week our cookbook came out, after two months of posting photos of recipes from it every day online, offering special PDFs of new recipes for people who preordered the book, sending notes to friends and asking them to help, it was the seventh-bestselling cookbook in America. I burst into tears when I read that email. And then I cried again when I read the next line: "You have to keep up this pace."

I had lost my desire to find licensing deals or do another run of the flour. The bread deal had fallen through after months of working on-site at the bread factory. The hope of my future bliss was diminishing. And even if it did arrive, I was no longer sure this pretending was worth the final goal.

Two months later, our daughter had a second skull surgery, only a three-hour surgery this time, to patch two holes in her skull that had never fused. The next week, she was fit with her first pair of hearing aids. Weeks later, at high altitude in Colorado, I developed pneumonia. Two weeks after that, our robustly healthy toddler son developed severe croup and needed a trip to the hospital.

As you might imagine, the medical bills of these events left us scrambling for work, scared that we might go bankrupt. I spent most of my days doing things I'm not good at, actions that aren't my passion—*Learn how to use Snapchat! Do more SEO work! Figure out how to compensate for the changes in the Facebook algorithms that mean only 3 percent of followers see our posts! Start another YouTube channel! Wait, now it's not Snapchat, it's Instagram Stories! Find more followers!*—to ensure that we could earn a living for our family. There was so little time to do what we love in the lives we were living.

We didn't have a steady job between us. We didn't know much about business. And we really didn't want to do what this path would require: give up our creative passions to make this work. Our friends who ran successful food businesses told us about the years and years they made everything by hand, did it themselves, and sold small and local. They went years without a sustainable salary or a vacation. Or even a day off. The greatest hope was to get the product in a few stores, then go bigger, all while working a full-time day job to pay the bills and have health insurance. Their dream was to go big enough to quit the job one day, then sell the business to a bigger company. Danny and I were both exhausted thinking of it all. We didn't want to hire a sales team, go to conferences around the country and sit in a booth and make appearances to sell the flour to a few more distributors, or take on investors to help us produce more flour. He wanted to cook. I wanted to write. We wanted to be with our kids.

. . .

And then, it was early December 2016. Like so many people in America, we were shell-shocked after the election. I couldn't, for the life of me, figure out how my creating more gluten-free muffin recipes would help anyone. But we barely had time to process it, since November is always the busiest month for a gluten-free business. Thanksgiving. Holiday baking. People ordering flour in droves. We were down to the last couple thousand boxes of flour and we wanted them gone. So we did one last push to sell out. I noticed that our business bank account was dwindling. That was strange, since we had so many orders in that three-week period. However, I barely had time to breathe, much less investigate it. Then, just after Thanksgiving, I went to our website, deep in the bowels of the e-commerce portion, to figure it out. I saw all the orders we had fulfilled, with the names and details, and a little spinning circle saying PENDING. In a panic, I wrote to our web developer. He investigated and found that between October 25 and December 1, we received hundreds and hundreds of flour orders and the shipping details as usual, then sent them out, like we had been doing for almost two years. But in all that time, no one's credit card had been processed, thanks to a technical glitch in the commerce site we were using. We had paid for all that shipping out of our own pocket. We had sent away nearly all of the last of our flour for free.

As Nicole Byer likes to say in *Nailed It*, "You're DONE!" We were done.

And it was a relief. I mean, don't get me wrong. There were a *lot* of tears and panic in those days. We sent out notices about what had happened. A few people sent us money. Most ignored it. We were out more than $4,000 and we did not have that money to spare.

However, there was relief in knowing this was not the right path for us. We had veered away from our greatest passions, the places where we felt like we were most alive in the world. We had exhausted ourselves in the hope that one day we could be at rest, no longer worrying about money. I didn't want to work so hard so that someday our lives could be as simple as they once were. Danny and I realized that we had not been equal in our marriage for years—me always the researcher, the decider, the one in charge, and he in the background cooking and running carpool for the kids. I wanted to be with him. I wanted to stop competing with everyone else who wrote cookbooks, especially the gluten-free ones. I wanted time off and more laughter. I no longer cared if our cookbooks made the best-seller list. I just wanted to rest.

• • •

After my ministroke, I did a lot of thinking. A lot of writing. I realized that wishing for more—an empire, recognition, so much money we would never have to worry again—is a ruse. It is only security we so desperately seek. And there is no such thing as security.

(I also now know that it is a hell of a lot easier to be a successful entrepreneur if you have a trust fund first.)

We were so afraid of running out of money that we took on a career path that didn't suit us at all. And we were really pretty awful at it. For years, I bought the same lie everyone else does: bliss is having lots of money and never having to worry. However, reaching for that future place of stasis meant we stopped following what fueled us. We stopped listening to our curiosity. We reached for the stars when all we wanted was our feet on the ground, holding hands together, our healthy kids by our sides.

It took Danny and I all that work and failure to realize we had already been living an extraordinary life in ordinary days. We have two small children, one of whom nearly died at birth, the other who took us years to find. After we quit the flour business, and then our blog, I found that all I wanted was time with my kids and my husband, our friends, our community. I wanted more time to walk in nature, where I always feel whole. I wanted more conversations with my women friends. I wanted days off. I did not want to be the head of an empire. I wanted to write.

I have my own definition of bliss now, not the consumer-capitalist conquering one. For me now, bliss is the feeling of being fully alive—the way I felt on that sidewalk in Paris long ago—then opening my eyes and wanting everyone around me to experience that too. We are for each other, not merely for ourselves.

I'm glad we did it (I think) even though just writing about it has given me a fierce stomachache. I buy at a local small business every chance I get. I'm proud of how hard

we both worked. We are grateful to the friends who wo[r]
with us and put up with our shenanigans. (How many ti[mes]
did I listen to the Beatles song "Drive My Car" and yet
I still enacted it?) And we tried. Oh, we tried. We failed,
spectacularly. I never did get that biscotti out. And in that
failure, I found out that I can be really, truly terrible at
something and still end up alive. I no longer need people
to *pick me, pick me!*

Mostly
Enough

TIME TO PREP THE DOUGHNUTS

I arrive at six in the morning, two hours before the store opens. Awaiting me is an aisle of boxes, stacked up. One last sip of my coffee, then I put on my gloves and take a big breath. Time to go in. I lug boxes, slash open tops with my cutter, put new packages of whole-grain seeded bread, naan, and seasonal sugar cookies on the shelves, and then haul the overstock to the back freezer. It takes me nearly an hour to stack all the boxes in the right places, label them, and leave the freezer clean. Then I walk to the bakery department and make sure the doughnuts are glazed and set in the case, waiting. By eight o'clock, when the store opens, I have made an inviting space for the first customers. At ten, during my lunch break, I meet my husband at the sports bar down the street for a plate of hash browns, sausages, and eggs over easy. I am hungry. I have worked hard.

I am a James Beard Award–winning gluten-free cook-book author. And for nine months, I worked in our local grocery store for fifteen dollars an hour.

It is the best job I have ever worked.

Online, no one knows you are poor. No one is posting photos of the basket of bills overflowing, some of the envelopes with URGENT stamped on them. Very few people write about the choices they make out of fear of going bankrupt, like selling expensive camera lenses that feel less important than rent. And few of us want to admit that we are struggling with money, even though we live in a culture where the rich have grown astronomically rich and the rest of us have grown anxious about health insurance. As my friend Ashley Ford wrote online one day, "I'm trying to choose an insurance plan, but I'm pretty sure the only good insurance is wealth."

I never shared online the time that Danny and I looked at our bank account and saw eighty-five dollars left for the last week of the month. We didn't have a savings account. We didn't have a 401(k) to drain for emergency funds. I had already done that eight years before. Our credit score was shot by the medical bills we couldn't pay after Lucy's terrifying time and the hospital stay for my ministroke. We had only eighty-five dollars and no way to charge anything on a credit card. Luckily, we were expecting a $6,000 check from a freelance gig, but it had been delayed. Still, we were like most Americans—living paycheck to paycheck (almost eight out of ten Americans, according to reputable studies) and unable to pay for an unexpected bill of more than $500 (nearly six out of ten Americans). We were struggling. And we were terrified. I realized that the mindset of worrying that we might go broke was damaging us.

I was no longer interested in following my bliss. I wanted to pay my bills.

Several artist friends recommended I find a manual labor job, one that would require none of my mind. I had never worked a job that merely asked me to show up. I found out that working part-time at the grocery store—three days a week—would give me health insurance for the entire family. And maybe putting premade pies on a display table would give me some time to think. So the next time I took a case of our gluten-free flour mix into our grocery store, I delivered an invoice and a job application. They hired me that week.

They put me in the bakery. Since I have celiac, I can't eat even a bit of gluten. But the bakery section in the grocery store is almost all packages, and I'm not allergic to plastic. It was a bit of a shock, at first, not being able to stop what I was doing to work on an essay or take photographs. Or check Twitter. After years of being a freelancer, I couldn't believe how wild my mind was when asked to do a task and then check back with my supervisor (a former student of mine) to ask what task she wanted me to complete next. I noticed that my mind balked. I kept working. And after a few weeks of shelving bags of croutons and cleaning out the cake case, I started to enjoy the wildness of my mind. At the store, I had to show up on time, do my work, then leave it all behind. I didn't know work could be that easy.

Friends came into the store and we would talk in three-minute bursts as I stocked frozen pizzas. Customers asked me questions about where we kept that one brand of whole-wheat bread, since it was the only one their kids would eat. I answered dozens of little questions a day. I realized that I liked feeling useful.

And all day long, I saw people, in tiny bantering interactions and questions. I developed a daily routine with fellow employees: a check-in at the cheese counter, a quick conversation about politics in produce. I would never have met any of these people I came to like, any other way. I started to feel like part of the community of my town.

On my lunch hours, I sat at the front of the store, taking notes. On the backs of papers that read "Grain-free flatbread, $6.49 each," I started writing lists. I look back at them now and realize I was clearing my mind of how I had lived. I wrote lists of what I wanted to accomplish in our house, our medical appointments, our taxes. I jotted down ideas for how to let go of *Gluten-Free Girl*. And I started taking notes on what I noticed about customers who had less money than most.

I noticed that the people who lived on the day-old breads looked around furtively to make sure no one saw when they reached into the discount bin. I led one woman to the back of the store to find the package of day-old rolls I had put in there, the gravy packets on sale, and some croutons for stuffing. "Thank you!" she said before she put her arms around me. "I'm going to have Thanksgiving because of you."

I found out that 22 percent of all students in our community's schools qualified for free or reduced lunches. That didn't account for the 10 percent of families who were above the official poverty line but still scrambling, or the single people or couples who did not have enough. That meant that nearly one out of three people who came into the store struggled to make ends meet.

Each day, at about two, I walked to the back freezer with a laminated list and a tall cart. I pulled boxes down from the top of the back freezer. Methodically, with plastic gloves on, I pulled the doughnuts—raspberry filled, Bavarian cream, chocolate glazed—and put them on black trays in a specified pattern. I was in the freezer by myself, pulling the doughnuts, humming a little. And then I wheeled the cart to the cooler, ready for the morning crew to bake them the next day.

Years before, I would have disdained these doughnuts: full of sugar, premade months before in a factory.

In the second year of my blog, I wrote a silly little piece about how Danny and I stood in line at the store and wondered at the crap in other people's carts. I received emails telling me I was being a food snob. At first defensive—*come on, America eats lousy food!*—I came to understand how wrong I had been. A woman shared with me how little she makes on her teaching salary in Oklahoma, how she visits the food bank to make it, and how a trip to the grocery store for cheap cake is an experience only reserved for once in a while when she can't stand the shame anymore. I was chastened and changed. And now I try to do better. How do I know that the woman buying the ninety-nine-cent doughnuts at our store isn't giving her two kids the only treat she can afford that week? And who am I to say that they shouldn't eat those doughnuts?

One day, I had a long conversation with the store's owner. At eighty-nine years old, he had owned the store for fifty-three years. His grandson had taken over managing the store, but the owner still clocked in twenty hours a week. Mostly, he spent that time in the city, at a store in a low-income neighborhood. He consulted a list of the twenty top-selling foods at our store. If the price in the city was lower, he called his grandson and told him to lower the price on ours. I stopped him one day to thank him for all that he did for our community. He told me, "It befuddles me that people put their focus on what is happening across the country and the world. There is enough to do here."

A few months after I started working there, I switched away from the bakery to bagging groceries. I loved the rhythm of fitting in food like a Jenga game. I have a lot of friends on the island. People who recognized me from my website came through my line. It took me a while to stop talking so much and focus on my work instead. (The assistant manager had to reprimand me in his office for that. I learned fast.) So I had the chance to do what I have always loved most: observe people when they're not watching me.

I learned that very few people make the highly styled dishes offered on Instagram. Oh sure, about every two weeks someone would come through with a bag full of vegetables, determined to juice for thirty days to lose weight. A few people bought jo-jo potatoes from the deli and an energy drink. But both of these were the outliers. Instead, most people bought meats, cheeses, some fruits and vegetables, three to five packaged crunchy foods, cat litter, toilet paper, beverages, butter, pads, and some kind of sweet thing or two. Maybe three people a day were buying ingredients for a specific recipe. Over and over, I saw that what my fellow recipe developers and I hashed out to make ourselves relevant—*Vegan treats for the whole family! How to use hempseed!*—was not being made in most homes. It humbled me.

I started paying attention to the people who shopped for the entire week with a plan. I took note of their food as I bagged it and how much it cost. I compared it to the people—like my husband and me—who shopped at the last moment. We were spending too much money on food. I started buying our meat from the discount bin and giving ourselves a limit on how much money we could spend each day. Our grocery bill started to grow smaller. Shopping was no longer a decadent pleasure for us but a mindset for being able to cook and eat without stress.

I left the job, eventually, because another opportunity worth more money walked into my path. And then, when that fell through, the next step arrived. Danny is the one working three days a week now, expediting in a restaurant, mostly for the connection with our community. I no longer earn any money online. When I go back to the store, every Sunday, my daughter skipping next to the cart, I hug my friends who work there. As I pass the front counter on my way out, I remember the urgency of those lunch-hour breaks—writing notes on the backs of recycled sale signs, where I first imagined the idea, then created the structure, and jotted down some of the first sentences for this book.

IN PRAISE OF ACQUAINTANCESHIP

I saw him most mornings when I drove to my teaching job. A man in combat fatigues, hulking as he walked down the side of the road, a machete in one hand, the other one out with his thumb up. As I passed him, I always wondered about his story.

Everyone had a Cool Gary story. He was hard to miss. Nearly every day, he walked up and down the main highway, looking for rides into town and back. The few people I knew who had picked him up said he was silent, grunting sometimes, but never mean or violent. When they reached town, he opened the door, mumbled a thanks, and walked off to wherever he was going. The first year I lived there, I was scared. How did we let a man with a machete walk up and down the highway? By the second year, I knew more of his story. Some said he had schizophrenia. Some said he had been in Desert Storm. He lived in the woods, near his mother. He never hurt anyone. There were people looking out for him without him knowing. So many wanted to take him in, to get him a home. But in the end, the kindest act seemed to be to leave him alone, since he wanted to live like that. As I passed him most mornings, I raised my hand in a wave. He always shook his machete at me for not giving him a ride.

Then when I moved to New York, I saw plenty of people talking to themselves on subway platforms, homeless men with hardened bare feet sleeping on the streets, and women with filthy hair wandering while coughing. I wondered if anyone cared for them. I wondered about their stories too. I would think of Gary often, how fully he was accepted. Whenever someone new came into town, and said, "But there's a man with a machete!" we all shrugged and said, "Yeah, that's Gary."

One morning in New York, I woke to an email from an island friend. Early the day before, Gary had been walking on the side of the highway in the fog. Some say he jumped in front of the car. Others said the car slid on slick road. Either way, Gary was dead. As soon as I read it, I started sobbing. So long, Cool Gary.

• • •

When I was a kid, I longed for friends. I was gawky and socially awkward, perpetually feeling like a cardboard cutout moving through a crowd of fully fleshed people. I yearned to go to other people's homes, or on field trips without my parents chaperoning, or kick around the neighborhood on my bike—the entire afternoon winding its way from one happy moment to another, without any need to mark it. And so whenever I did have a chance to connect with people, I wanted depth. I wanted to move immediately from the first few lines of conversation to fast friends. Thank goodness for my two friends, Mike and Sharon, who saved me from total loneliness. But the paucity of casual conversations, combined with the ferocity of my sadness and desire for connections, made me terrible at talking with people for years.

Have you ever been to a party where a group of you are standing around in a circle, laughing about nothing much? And then someone comes up, eyes wide open, and insists everyone else move a little to make room for her? As you try to turn back to the source of laughter, a little fractured now, she looks at one person in the circle and says, "Hey, what are you guys talking about?" That was me. Sincere. Earnest. And completely baffled about how to successfully negotiate any social interaction.

Thousands of frozen conversations, stutter-step conversations like the drip of water falling off icicles, and finally conversations like warm water running over rocks taught me how to step back and relax. Somehow I have been friends with Sharon for thirty-six years, Tita and Gabe for twenty-six. The awkward girl who had no friends now has more than she can count. I have a dozen friends whom I could call at two in the morning in an emergency, knowing they would pick up the phone.

Once I had a pool of people I could rely on, I stopped searching every new face for signs of my salvation. And once I met my husband, I stopped searching every new face for signs I would be loved. The search fell away, revealing who I could be without that frantic energy. I could meet people for who they were, not what they could do for me.

When my daughter was first born, I kept a food blog that thousands of people were reading. I talked all through the day with people whose handles I recognized on Twitter, Facebook, and then Instagram. I felt gratified to know that my writing meant something to people. I was thrilled every time someone wrote to say she had made our recipe for her family. However, it turns out that talking with people on the computer was an eerie simulation of my time as a kid. I was helping people, answering their questions through a screen. In reality, I was spending a lot of time alone, by myself with a toddler. *Gluten-Free Girl* was an online figment, something I could have created in any town. I was a resident of the small island community where we lived, but I didn't live there. Somehow I had recreated the loneliness of my mother's life when my brother and I were small.

When I found the courage to try to find my own definition of *enough*, I realized that I didn't have enough people in my life. Oh, I had my wonderful husband, my daughter and son, my two or three closest friends. But that wasn't enough.

. . .

S*esame Street* debuted on television two years after I was born, so it's no surprise that certain songs are tattooed on my brain. Every day, I still hear Bob saying, "You know, there are all kinds of interesting people that live right around your neighborhood." He talks with the grocer—who offers Bob kale!—the doctor, the postman, the firefighter, the baker. And even though I'm lucky enough to keep making new friends I adore, I notice that it's the people in my neighborhood, the people that I meet each day, who mean the most to me these days.

At the thrift store, my son goes straight to the toy section, where three buddies are playing. I move my cart to the kitchen section, where plates are fifty cents each. I stop to arrange a playdate with the mother of a friend of my daughter's. We set the playdate and move away. The woman who used to be in charge of the domestic violence advocacy group on the island is in the book section, so we stop to discuss the local political campaign she is coordinating. Back in the clothes section, the woman who leads a performance art troupe with her husband is reaching for a pair of red boots. We stop to make plans to visit the upcoming market run by the Syrian families who moved to the island. One of their daughters has become good friends with our girls. We check out with the woman who always shouts cheerfully to my son, "How you doing, D?" She has worked at this community thrift store—organized almost entirely by volunteers, with profits given to organizations in our community like the senior center, food bank, and health clinic—for more than a decade. For the past six years, I've played softball with her twin adult daughters, who raise guide dogs for the blind. We joke and laugh with her every Thursday afternoon, my boy and I. I've never seen her outside of the store.

Desmond and I stop at the grocery store on the way to pick up his sister at school. We only need a few things— grapes, salami, a bag of gluten-free pasta—but I've planned a full thirty minutes for the trip. In front of the olive bar, the woman who does cooking demos waves hello to Desmond. I discuss the latest game with the butcher who used to be a baseball coach. I stop at the bakery department to get Desmond a free cookie and talk with my former supervisor.

In produce, we run into the man who owns the
our favorite ferry worker, and Lucy's ballet teacher.
talk with my favorite checker and wave hello to the
girl passing by, the one who makes Italian sodas for us
coffee stand. Desmond and I wave to our favorite bank ꞔꞔer
across the parking lot as she walks into the store.

Those interactions are never longer than five minutes.
They don't need to be. I'm grateful for all of them.

• • •

I'm grateful for the common humanity I find in my
community. Many of the people I see in our errands are
enigmas to me. I don't know their politics or their childhood
experiences or the way they deal with stress. They may not
be the kinds of folks who would be my closest friends. We
don't have the same sense of humor or love of food or
persistent grit. I think. What do I know? All I do know is
that I need them in my life as much as my closest friends.
Maybe even more. A slew of recent studies from places
like Harvard Health and the National Institutes of Health
suggest that having a plethora of social interactions in your
life helps you to live longer and enjoy better health. Those
connections—fleeting, repeating—might be more important than eating well, exercising, or even quitting smoking.
Life is long, if you're lucky. And it seems that having a lot of
people you know by sight, to whom you give a quick wave
or take a meal after a new baby is born, is a darned fine way
to live a long life.

When I see the people in my neighborhood, chatting and
connecting for a few moments, I feel alive to the world. I am

more than my to-do list, my weight, my bank account. I'm part of my community.

And my community is made of fully fleshed people, not the cardboard cutouts of online personas. The couple that sells salmon to us out of their shack on the side of the road—he grumbles under his breath about political ideas that make me wince; she is deeply religious. And she adores my kids. We buy our Christmas tree from them every year. They are real to us. Different than us. Dear to us.

After being trapped inside my head, in the mindset of my mother for decades, it's a relief to have a quick chat with someone in the middle of the street during our small town's Halloween celebrations and need nothing more. I'm larger for having these people in my life.

• • •

Students I taught twenty-five years ago have come back to our town as adults in their forties. It's wild to have these people in my life again, this time as parents to my kids' friends. I look at three-year-olds and know that, life willing, I will watch them graduate high school one day.

My guess is that the kids of the kids of the kids I once taught in the early '90s will pass the wooden sculpture on the side of the highway on our island and ask a familiar question. "Mama, why is there a statue of a guy with sunglasses holding a machete right there?"

And that mama, driving her daughter to school, will say, "Well, my love, a long time ago, there was a man in our community named Cool Gary . . . "

And so the story will go on.

FALLING IN LOVE
WITH WOMEN

I slide into the booth and fling my purse on the bench. My head is swimming with lists of things to do and essays to write. Across the table from me sits my friend Tina, who has a laptop and papers splayed out in front of her. We look at each other, then shrug, and then we start to laugh.

"Hi you," she says.

"Hi you," I tell her. "How's your day?"

"Well," she says, laughing, her shoulders hunching to her ears. "The usual shitshow. You?"

I laugh out loud. I can feel the tension in my back easing. "Oh, just fine and dandy!"

We order coffee and food, then shove our work to the other side of the table to make room for our plates. And each other. She tells me the news of the past week: teenage son with ADHD trying to contemplate the SATs; other teenage son bursting in a hormonal bout; daughter sassy and butting heads with someone at school; fisherman husband coming home angry after a not-great crab season. And me?

Book due soon; the website I'm creating for a local business needs to launch this week; darling daughter so besotted with her musical theater production she can't pay attention in math; four-year-old son and husband butting heads, again. The elections. And I haven't gone for a walk in a week, or bathed for a few days, plus I have a headache.

We're talking fast, interrupting each other with consolation exclamations, and gesturing so widely that I nearly smack our server when she brings my Caesar salad. We laugh again, then dive into our food. Everything feels lighter already.

I wend my way around sentences about how it will all be more spacious soon, and I've been through this before, and I'm sure I'll feel fine next week. Tina looks at me and says, "You know, sometimes I feel like you are spectacularly good at taking care of yourself, and other times I think you are good at talking about it and spectacularly bad at actually doing it."

I blurt out something reassuring to myself and her, then stop. I think for a moment, chewing. So few people know how to cut through the chase of me and say that.

"Yeah, you're right," I say. "This might be a talking time instead of a doing time."

She nods, then takes a sip of her soup. "I mean, I know this one."

"Yep," I say. "You're talking to yourself here too, aren't you?"

"Damned straight!" she says, and we laugh again.

I want to reach across the table and hug her, but there's no need to get salad dressing on my coat. She knows.

• • •

For the first few decades of my life, I was perpetually wary of women. Girls in elementary school confused me with their mean-girl games and two-faced behavior. Of course, there were quiet girls, tomboys, math whizzes, and nontraditional girls at my schools, but I wasn't allowed to spend more time with them to find out who they were beneath their exteriors. So I observed the mass of them, as I sat under a tree on the playground, reading but also studying their ways like a scientist behind a bluff watching wild animals at work. After fourth grade, when puberty hit, all those feminine wiles intensified. And I tried, I tried so hard, to fit in with them. I remember the long minutes every morning trying to make my straight-ass hair do the Farrah Fawcett flip and failing. In seventh grade, my parents bought me an original pair of Nikes, after I begged. But somehow, the blue ones with the yellow swoop weren't as cool as the white ones with the red swoop. One summer every girl in Southern California was wearing OP shorts—those super flimsy high-cut surfer shorts, meant for slim thighs and a flat stomach. I stuffed my legs into them and felt they looked like sausages flopping out of their casings. For a few weeks, I was certain that Bonne Bell Dr Pepper lip gloss would save me. It didn't.

I always felt like I was performing femininity to fit in and find friends. Since I was on the outside looking in, I devoted as much of my energy as I could to making sense of it all. It seemed that the girls who were the most successful were the ones who looked the best, because the boys liked them. Makeup and clothes and boys! Oh my. No matter how hard I tried to understand it, I remained mystified. So I gave up.

All my acquaintances and banter partners were boys. They seemed so much more real. They wanted to play baseball and make movies and have board game tournaments. This I understood. And their talks—wisecracking, nothing too emotional—also made sense to me. Since I refused to wear a dress until I was seventeen, I fit right in. I was a geeky tomboy, shy and sometimes ridiculous. All the geeky guys liked me and made me feel like I belonged. Then again, I was perpetually saddened when they thought of me as friend material, not a girlfriend. Not really a boy and not welcomed by the girls. Story of my life.

If I had not been socially stunted the first twenty-nine years of my life, perhaps I would have been able to look around and find other women like me: tomboys who loved musicals and thick books, softball and searching talks; *Monty Python* fans who were happy in nature; introverts who liked adventures on a limited basis. I didn't find them until my forties.

Even though I had lots of individual women friends through my thirties, it wasn't until I gave birth that I fell in love with women. Carrying my daughter deep in my body softened me. After giving birth to her, and especially after adopting another mother's son, I look at every face I pass and think, *You are the son or daughter of a mother.* Mothers create the world. And I find it impossible to hate anyone, based on that knowledge.

Even though my daughter's first few weeks of life terrified me, I came through the terror. I realized that I was made of tougher stuff than I had thought when I was in my twenties, passive and perpetually trying to please my mother. Now I *am* the mother. And I am stronger for all the broken places. I know that I love my daughter and son fiercely.

I will protect them, but I will also let them fall and make mistakes and fully be in the world. Sometimes I am a jam-stained jungle gym, but I'm still a woman. Becoming a mother made me braver. It made me stronger. It made me love being a woman.

Every woman with whom I connect is tough—running businesses, a little driven, unafraid of failure—and has a soft heart dedicated to helping other people. Sam runs the bakery and creamery in our town. She's always dealing with employee problems, walk-ins that break, a flood, a sick kid, and still producing food to feed our community. So does Jen, who owns the burger and ice cream place, admitting freely that this shit ain't easy, all with a giant smile. Melinda has been running the restaurant in the center of town for thirteen years, creating community with grit, grace, and incredible energy. Margo, my marvelous friend with the wide-open heart, recreates her life as she goes, as an artist and mother. Tamiko thinks deeply about every action she takes, making words into sentences that move others with their honesty. Kim runs a three-ring circus in her home with two tween girls and two younger siblings adopted from foster care, negotiating their learning needs and writing about it all freely. Krissy is the mother of seven, a homeschooler—oh, I could *never*—and she deeply understands every single kid and fights for each one. Lynne endured the discovery that her husband had been cheating on her for a year, then soon after was diagnosed with breast cancer, and survived it all with her deep belly laugh, because what else are you going to do? These are the women who dive in, get their hands dirty, and insist on the details instead of spouting opinions. They make me feel good when I am with them. These are the women who do not pretend.

Now that I have them, and I have stopped pretending, I look back at all the popular girls, the pretty girls, the girls who knew how to play the girl game, and I want to hug them all. How much struggle could have been in every one of them? Who knows what their stories were? I hope that they have found their women friends who do not pretend.

I do know that if I had been socially adept and able to find my women friends earlier, I would have very different friends now. I love my women. I found my people by dint of my grit and my ability to let go.

It wasn't until I started writing this book that it occurred to me: of course I was wary of women when I was raised by the mother to whom I was born. Time. Everything takes time and persistence, especially when it comes to seeing yourself clearly.

• • •

As I enter fully into my fifties, I love my husband dearly. My children are very much the heart of my life. But when it comes to the place where I feel most fully a woman, it's in the company of my good women friends who don't give a fuck about what society wants from them anymore.

I can't wait to see what it feels like when I'm in my seventies.

GOOD-ENOUGH MOTHER

We sit down at the table together, the early morning light falling through the smudged windows. Lucy scrunches her nose. "Mama, Daddy brought me my least-favorite yogurt." She holds up the offending blueberry container. I look over at Danny, and we look right into each other's eyes a beat longer than usual. "Lucy, eat your yogurt," I tell her. "You may prefer lemon but you have this one. And you're lucky." She harumphs into her shoulders but I ignore it. She's hungry.

Desmond is flying two little plastic superhero figures in the air, making noises. "D," I tell him. "Time to eat. Dada made you scrambled eggs." He doesn't listen. I reach over and touch his shoulder lightly. "Buddy, time to eat." He looks up and says, "But Mama, I'm not hungry. They have to get the bad guys. I can't stop to eat." He goes back to his toys.

I take a breath, then go in. "Honey, remember, there is no such thing as bad guys. Just people who were hurt and made a lot of bad choices, over and over." He looks at me. He's four. He has heard me say this for two years and he has come to accept it. When he's talking with other kids, I will hear him say, "Those guys made bad choices." But in front of me, he wants nothing to do with it. There are invisible bad guys hanging over the table, and his good guys are going to get them. Besides, steam still billows up from the eggs. I put my hand on his shoulder and hold it there. "Kiddo, Superman and Batman are hungry too. Put them next to the plate and let them eat. They're going to have more strength if they have food." Desmond lines up the guys close to each other, in meticulous precision. He turns toward his eggs.

Danny and I both take sips of lukewarm coffee and shake our heads, grinning at each other. "Okay, guys, it's time." And so we sing together, the little nondenominational song we made up years ago. "Amen! Amen! Amen, amen, amen!" They both sing it, loudly, sometimes in harmony, with gusto.

"Lucy, what are you grateful for?"

She looks up from her graphic novel—she loves reading so much that we compromised and gave her permission to read at breakfast, except when we want to hear from her or have her listen—and says, "I'm grateful that I have rehearsals for *Mary Poppins* today. We're doing the chimney sweep song!"

I ask her about it, then ask her when she needs costumes. Since she's forgetful, perhaps more than most ten-year-olds, I make a note on the slip of paper I keep beside my plate to email her director and get all the dates. She goes back to her book.

"Desmond, what are you grateful for today?"

He looks up, starts to talk, and then stops when he notices that I have seen his mouth is full. He swallows. "School!" he says. "I'm going to play and play and play."

"Yeah buddy!" Danny says to him. I make a note on the paper—find D a new pair of rain boots.

"Hey honey," I ask Danny. "What are you grateful for?"

He takes a sip of the coffee, then looks at the kids. "I'm grateful that I'm going to work today. I'm really loving it lately."

Lucy asks him about the restaurant, the place where she plans on being a server when she is in high school. These two are so alike. They think best when their feet are dancing. They live in exuberance, unable to plan ahead or remember their coats, loving and wonderful. They have incredible palates, they are terrible spellers, and they both teach me, constantly. My daughter relies on me to schedule her life to keep it sane. She comes to me when she has questions and knows that I will nudge her when she answers my questions with a tight "fine." We both love movies, books, and baseball with equal passion, and I imagine years of shared time singing show tunes in the car. But her dad is so much like her that they have an indelible bond, something unspoken. They understand each other. I love watching them together.

Desmond puts his hand on my arm. "What are you grateful for, Mama?" I smile down at him, this little whirlwind of questions and sly sense of humor. His brain works like mine: thinking in large patterns, structuring life as he goes, asking questions always. He said to me one day, "Mama, why does everything drop to the ground? I've been noticing and nothing floats up into the air. Why is that? Why does it all drop down?"

He was four.

I looked at him in the rearview mirror, saw his eyes intently waiting. "Well, what you are describing is a force called gravity. It's what propels everything toward the center of the earth."

He looked out the window, thinking, and then said, "Okay. But why does it do that?"

I was lost. Has anyone understood that? Certainly not me. And my daughter never asked these questions, so I had no easy answer. "Buddy, that's a good, big question. I don't know the answer. And when you go to MIT someday, you'll be surrounded by people who ask questions like that." That seemed to satisfy him.

This kid keeps us on our toes.

He also bristles at the tags on the backs of shirts, flinches at loud noises, and explodes with too much energy when he is overstimulated by being in a room with too many people. (He once told me, "Mama, I don't want to be in a room with more than eighteen people.") We manage our expectations of the places we can take him, the kinds of experiences he might be able to handle. Desmond adores his island preschool, where he spends most of his time outdoors with his friends, building forts and fording streams together, then going inside to learn how to draw letters in the sand and identify the birds they saw that day. But take him to the library with too many people in it and he is climbing the backs of couches, swinging the green alligator puppet at my chest when I try to grab him. It's a constant dance, helping this one walk through the world.

I'm happy to be dancing with him, with them.

So when Desmond puts his hand on my arm and asks me what I am grateful for that day, I look around the room. I see the cookbooks splayed open where Danny left them after looking for a new brine recipe for last night's roast chicken. I see Lucy's playbook on the floor, Legos spilling out of their drawer, crayons on the table by a drawing with a ring of coffee stain on it. I look into the kitchen and see the dishes that need doing, the calendar on the wall stuffed with events. And I feel the headache from staying up too late writing, after doing a full day's work and getting the kids to bed. I tilt my head toward the window and see the sun shining on the trees, shimmering with orange leaves about to fall to the ground.

I turn back to my family and hold Desmond's hand. "This, buddy. I'm grateful for all of this."

• • •

For about a decade, I didn't know if I wanted to be a mother. My twenties were so miserably dark in large part because I felt beholden to my mother, taking care of her, propping her up. In my mind, I had already been a part-time parent for her, and for my father who did so little to help us, that I didn't want to take it on again. When I lived in New York, I walked the streets feeling free, unencumbered by the need to take care of another person in the world. I still think of that feeling sometimes, when I'm picking up clothes off the floor, putting the plastic dump truck outside, and facing the dishes again. I still miss it, once in a while.

However, something shifted after those years in New York. When I was about thirty-three, that thing kicked in. *Must have babies.* Since there was no man in my life yet, it was entirely theoretical, this pulsing desire to be a mother somehow. So I had a lot of time to think about it. Eventually, I realized that I didn't want the way I was raised to take away my chance to know my children. It had been hard, so damned hard. But life is long. And I deserved more.

Long before, when I was in college, I circled a passage in a psychology book so many times that I nearly obliterated the words. It was written by a British psychologist and pediatrician named D. W. Winnicott. I sat up straight the first time I read his observations. "The good-enough mother . . . starts off with an almost complete adaptation to her infant's needs, and as time proceeds she adapts less and less completely, gradually, according to the infant's growing ability to deal with her failure." I loved the notion that parenting inherently involved failure. Who on earth could be a perfect mother? Instead of pretending and pushing to be perfect, Winnicott advocated for the good-enough mother. And the passage I circled a dozen times was this image: Winnicott wrote that he could spot a good-enough mother if she was on one end of the room, doing something she loved, and her child was on the other end of the room, playing. They weren't talking. They were separate beings, together.

When I thought hard in my thirties about whether or not I wanted to be a mother, I remembered that image. That phrase—good-enough mother—echoed in my head, on repeat. After years of therapy and meditation, I hoped that I would not make the same mistakes my mother had made. Good enough? I thought I could do that. When I met Danny, I was ready to be an imperfect, generous, learning-as-I-go mother.

Unfortunately, so many people have come to believe that being a perfect mother means putting up the pretense of perfection and providing constant safety. When my daughter was two, she started to climb the ladder to the tall slide at the playground. She knew what she was doing. So I sat a few feet away, talking with a friend. And another mother jumped to stand under my daughter, her hands waiting in case she fell. She looked around to see who the negligent parent was, then glared at me. I applauded Lucy when she flew down the slide, delighted. "Great job, kiddo! Go try the swings."

My own mother still flinches with fear around my kids. When she and my father visit, and one of the kids falls down on the porch after running hard, my mom still pulls in her breath like she's yanking on a chain. I never react with fear to my kids' cuts and scrapes. I want them to stumble, then learn how to stand up and start dancing again. When my kids were younger, my mother would stand up and shout, "Oh no!" after a fall. They would start crying, assuming they must be hurt badly. Now, though, Lucy is old enough to know, "Oh, that's just Grandma."

I still keep my parents in my life. That might be a surprise. I'm trying to love them, to forgive them. One way I do that is to keep the boundaries clear. They insist they should be allowed to see my children every single Saturday, in a set procession from my brother's house (where they arrive at ten thirty on the dot), then to our house exactly at noon. We don't let it happen every Saturday, but we go through cycles where we see them most weeks. They bring lollipops and iPads, let the kids play games, stroke the kids' legs, and tell them how beautiful and wonderful they are. I go to the other room and find work to do. I'm no longer angry at them, not actively. It's easy for me to see how sad their lives are, how they have chosen social isolation and pretense for the rest of their days. I know now they did the best they could, in their own stunted way. They still won't acknowledge what happened when my brother and I were kids or apologize for how they behaved. Once in a while, they say something that sparks a smoldering in me. But I take a breath and clean the table, then wave as they walk out the door.

For years, my daughter loved those interactions. Now, she's starting to wonder why it is that her grandparents have never driven her anywhere, why her grandmother panics when Lucy wants to go outside for a walk in the woods with her cousin, and if they will ever stop doting on her so much.

Recently, she asked if she could take a break from the man-datory visits. She's ten. She wants to go on playdates with her friends or go to the museum or zoo on a Saturday. Mostly, though, she wants a little space to breathe. I agreed. I run interference with my parents and tell them we're busy one week or two. For an hour or so there will be a flurry of texts, imploring us to change our minds, asking when they can see the kids next, and accusing us of blocking them from their greatest joy. I don't engage. Eventually, the kerfuffle dies away.

Sometimes, about every three months, my mother blows up at me in anger for something I didn't see coming. One time, she paced around our home and shouted at me because I didn't want to gossip about why my second cousin invited my mother to her wedding. It didn't make much sense to me. I refused to engage. Essentially, even in this situation, I'm sitting on a bench, away from the fray, not getting involved. My commitment to family and keeping the connection going, in spite of the difficulty, doesn't mean I need to negotiate my mother's fear or my father's accusations of not being a good-enough daughter anymore. We'll see where the relationship goes when my kids are more grown.

All I can do is try to be a good-enough mother to my own kids.

• • •

The last year I taught high school, I received a phone call from the mother of one of my students. She invited me to a party they were throwing for their daughter, before she left for her senior year abroad in Denmark. I remarked on the incredible generosity of this parent, allowing her daughter to spend her last year of high school in another country, far away. After that, she would go to college. Most parents would cling.

And she told me a story. "You know, when my daughter was born, I looked at her and immediately felt flooded with love. When they put her in my arms, I whispered to her, 'I love you so much. And now I have to learn how to let you go.'"

I started sobbing, one of those uncontrollable pulses from deep in the throat. I hung up the phone and cried. My mother never told me that.

Lucy let out a loud, barbaric yawp when she was born, a giant squall that in photographs looks like she is singing. Yep. That's Lucy.

Desmond's birth mother asked me to be the first person to hold him, a gift I will always treasure, a story I have already told him several times to show him how much both of his mothers love him. And when they put him in my arms, I could feel the weight of his wisdom in his body. He stayed quiet, eyes open, looking at everything intently. We sat together for two hours as I whispered to him and sang to him and fed him. He looked right at me. He closed his eyes in pleasure when they washed his hair with warm water. And he only started to grow upset when another newborn came into the room, bawling. He turned his head toward the sound and his lip quivered. He was worried for her, the other newborn. I held him close and explained that sometimes there is sadness in the world. It would pass. It did.

Within a few moments of both my kids being born, I leaned down and kissed their foreheads and said, "I love you with all my heart. And now I have to learn how to let you go."

NEVER STEP ON THE SCALE AGAIN

One year to the day after my ministroke, I saw my doctor for a checkup. That year had been one of the most clarifying of my life. Because of his suggestion that I dig deeper into the intangible, to investigate where I did not feel good enough and how that had damaged me, I had to change my life. Danny and I had grown closer, more honest still. I scheduled time for walks and coffee with my friends first, then working at the computer after. Our family joined the gym where I had begun swimming, lifting weights, and committing to yoga. We let go of Gluten-Free Girl as our business. Our town had become the center of our world. We had come to terms with the idea that we might never have two stable jobs, since that's how our brains worked, and we would be creating our lives, then recreating them, over and over. Our kids were thriving. I started writing this book.

At the visit with my doctor, I was able to report that I was sleeping a consistent seven hours a night. My cholesterol numbers had improved and my blood pressure had dropped thirty points. I was, without a doubt, the healthiest I had ever been. And I weighed, to the pound, exactly what I had the day of the TIA.

So I took a breath and said to him, "You know, I think now that the year has passed, and I'm no longer worried a bigger stroke will strike, it's time for me to dive in and really lose some weight."

My empathetic doctor, who listened more deeply than any medical professional I have ever met, looked at me, took his own deep breath, and said, "Shauna, I don't think you're right. I think it's time for something different. I want you to never step on the scale again."

Shocked, I stared at him. How could that be true? Everything, everything in this culture told me I would never be truly healthy until I weighed below a certain weight. Every day, a new diet screamed onto the scene, promising the elixir of thin by urging us to cut carbs, stop eating meat, work more fat into our diets, eschew grains, or eat like cavemen. I had spent my entire life, from the age of ten on, living my days with a little stutter step in the back of my mind. *Yes, this is good, but think of how much better your life will be when you lose the weight. Then you will be whole.*

Dr. G had listened to me talk through my worries about my weight and health for years. Should I try vegan? Should I eat more protein? Less? Was my celiac an indicator for diabetes? If I lost fifty pounds, would I finally be well? For years, he had given me some pointers but no directives. He told me once about a film he had seen of a man, who lived as part of a tribe in a developing nation, climbing a tree. The man was patient and calm as the bees in the hive buzzed around his face. He climbed down the tree with a handful of honey, which he shared with his wife and three kids. "The way we uilt biologically, it should be that hard to get something et," he told me. But when I asked him if that meant I ould cut out sugar completely, he told me that wasn't the way either. Too much restriction brought up old habits in my mind—I swelled with sadness in my chest and ended up bursting out of it, eating all the cakes and cookies we were testing for our recipes. Could I live with some sugar in my life, with boundaries? That's what I had finally learned to do the year after the stroke. It helped that we had stopped making baked goods for our living.

Still, I had not lost a pound. When I told Dr. G that I was shocked he had suggested that my weight wasn't the point, he said something that changed my life again. "You can be the weight you are and be truly healthy. I want you to uncouple the idea of health and an ideal weight."

I blinked, lost for words.

Dr. G wrote down the name of a neuroscientist, Sandra Aamodt, who had recently published a piece in the *New York Times* he was suggesting all of his patients read: "Why You Can't Lose Weight on a Diet."

In that piece, as well as in her TED Talk, Aamodt explained that each person's brain has a weight-regulation system built in to determine the set point for our weight. Whether we go from 120 to 80 pounds, or from 300 to 200, our brain's response is to slow our metabolism and put a halt to that weight loss. Only 1 in 677 obese women will reach a "normal" weight within a year of dieting. Keeping it off is even harder. In a weight-loss industry report that Aamodt cited, 231 million Europeans tried dieting in 2002. Only 1 percent of those people lost weight and kept it off.

The system is rigged against us. In essence, dieting is a capitalist scam.

However, if weight is tied to health, then we have to persevere, train ourselves to not take pleasure in our food, and eat skinless boneless chicken breasts and steamed broccoli for the rest of our lives, right? Turns out, no. As my doctor, this neuroscientist writer, and many others have started to point out, the mere act of stepping on the scale, chastising ourselves, counting calories, and assigning our overweight selves the task of being less triggers the body to produce stress hormones, which increases the amount of fat cells in our bodies, which increases abdominal fat. It's dieting that is producing excess stress and fat.

"We're learning now, through many longitudinal and trustworthy studies, how little weight loss actually matters," my doctor told me. He admitted, honestly, that even he had been surprised the past few years to see the truth in action. According to the studies he had read and seen shared at many conferences, the highest early mortality rates occurred for the truly, morbidly obese. But the second group with high early mortality rates? The ultra-athletes, like the people who run hundred-mile races. It turns out that both groups are extreme. The middle way—as in most things—is far healthier.

Because we live in such a fat-shaming society, we all assume that too much weight is an automatic danger. However, it turns out that smoking, high blood pressure, not exercising, drinking too much alcohol, living under the stress of not enough money, and social isolation are more accurate predictors of early death than being overweight.

"I know this is different than anything you have ever read or heard, but your weight alone is not an indicator of your health," Dr. G said. "Look what has happened to you this year. You're calm. Your blood pressure is down. You feel like you have enough. What if that is enough? I want you to find out for yourself what *your* optimal health is. Never step on the scale again."

I walked away in a daze. Happy, confused, and unsure what to do. Except, I knew to trust my doctor. He had been there for me through my pregnancy, through Lucy's terrifying first couple weeks of life, through Danny's days of quitting alcohol, through my breast cancer scares, and through my TIA. He had consistently been a calm, scientific force in my life. Danny and I used to joke that we wanted to schedule appointments with Dr. G just to talk with him, since he was such a font of wisdom. Why not listen to him?

The first month after that talk, I watched myself. I noticed how I reached for a second piece of cake because I was never getting on the scale again. I ate sandwiches with thick inches of butter and salami. I took second and third helpings, since no one was watching and it wasn't my weight that determined my health. Sweet potato chips, pork cracklings, key lime pie for breakfast? Why not?

Within a month, I realized why not. I felt like shit. My skin was ragged and red. I wasn't sleeping well at night. My belly felt too full, all the time. My pants didn't fit. I was short of breath when I walked up too many stairs. This did not feel healthy.

Suddenly, freed from the societal notion of what I *should* be doing—dieting and worrying about every bite, measuring my success by becoming less of myself—I could finally hear my own body. Without a goal—*Lose fifteen pounds by wedding day! Be a smaller size by the time I need to buy clothes for the book tour!*—I was no longer holding my breath. I could no longer tell myself I would be starting to "eat right" the next day, so eat all the cheese I could see before me that night. If my health was entirely up to me, then I wanted to live better than I had been.

...

I know how American success stories are supposed to end. In a culture fueled by capitalism and suffused with misogyny, I should be telling you how I found the secret that placed me even more fully in the gaze of male adoration. So this is where I tell you that, at fifty-two, during perimenopause, in spite of not getting on the scale again, I managed to lose thirty pounds without trying!

Oh hell no. Nope. At my previous doctor's appointment, when they asked to weigh me, it turned out I weighed within three pounds of what I had weighed at that last appointment. That number—it's where my body wants to be.

I talked with my oncologist a couple of months after I talked with Dr. G. She's a blunt woman who is kind and knows more than I can imagine. In one of my yearly appointments, I asked her if there was anything I should be eating, or not eating, to prevent cancer. She told me that—contrary to popular opinion—the science isn't there for certain foods being demonized. "Don't smoke. We know that." (I don't.) "Don't drink much, if at all." But, she told me, eating superfoods from Brazil or avoiding tofu won't help. "Eat a lot of vegetables. No one argues that vegetables are bad for us. Exercise. A lot." And she told me essentially the same thing Dr. G had—weight alone is not an indication of health. "Look at every actress who is over fifty. If you look at Meryl Streep in her early twenties, she was rail thin. And now, in her sixties, she is pleasantly plump. She can afford trainers and chefs and people to tell her how to lose weight. But she's a woman. And women, as we age, we grow softer around the edges. It's the way of things."

Later, I talked with a friend of mine who is a nutrition-ist. I asked her why it is I always lost weight on vacation. Sure, I'm walking around a new city, but I walk often. And on vacation, I eat ice cream and charcuterie and anything I want. And yet, I would come home lighter. Why? "Oh, that's easy," she told me. "When you eat with any guilt or sense of doing something wrong, it releases cortisol in the body, which adds more abdominal fat. When you eat with joy, mindfully, happily around the table with friends? There's a hormonal response that speeds up your metabo-lism and helps you digest it all better." I thought of all the long dinners Danny and I ate on our honeymoon in Italy—gluten-free pasta, braised cuts of meat, prosciutto, and gelato. They were spread out over several hours, talking and gesticulating with new friends. That food felt different going down than an equal amount of "clean meals" of dutiful vegetables and lean meats.

It's possible that the secret to long life is to eat with friends, laughing, and to enjoy our food.

That's what I gained by deciding to listen to my body instead of stepping on the scale: freedom. I didn't lose pounds, I lost the restrictions I had put on my own happiness.

I finally let go of the notion that I would ever have an after photo, the shining side by side with the bloated former self that would prove to everyone in this society that I had been successful.

By listening to my body, I learned that, aside from gluten, I don't do well with dairy. Instead of numbers, I noticed the clog in my throat, the achy joints, my gut in knots. Man, I love cheese. But feeling healthy was more important than Havarti. Turns out after a couple of months without it, I didn't think about it much. And that was my biggest gift: to not have to think about food with anxiety again.

We eat well in our house. And without having to document our meals, or wonder aloud in midbite how to make it better when I write it down, I can slow down and enjoy what I eat. And how do I eat? Mostly a lot of vegetables. Lean meats and seafood. Some bacon sometimes. Lots of olive oil, with clarified butter for a bit of richness. Roasted tofu. Good dark chocolate, every night. I'm not afraid of carbs, but I notice when I eat too many empty ones, I feel sort of gross. So I'll have quinoa fritters for breakfast, or creamy polenta with braised pork and roasted vegetables, or white rice for a stir-fry. And on Saturdays—or when friends make me a gluten-free baked good—I eat a slice of pumpkin pie or savor coconut ice cream or enjoy that gingerbread cake with honey frosting. When Halloween rolls around, I'm no longer interested in eating my kids' candy. It doesn't taste good to me anymore.

And other than that, I really don't think about food. I love it in the moment. And then I let it go.

BREAKING THE GIRL CODE

Ask any woman in America and they could probably recite their list of things they hate about themselves. "Oh, I'm fine with my breasts but my butt is so big. I wish my thighs were smaller. I'd have given anything to have lips like yours." It really doesn't matter what is on that list. So many of us carry our lists in our pockets, weighing us down, bringing them out to share with other girls and women to say, "I do this too. I'm one of you."

If you ever have wondered why women still do not receive equal pay or why they have to endure a culture of sexual harassment and a lack of reproductive rights, it's because we were encoded from birth to make ourselves smaller and smaller.

It's what we have been taught, for decades, by magazine spreads, by television commercials, by the multitudes of thin white women under thirty who have been cast in television shows and movies for the past fifty years. We are not enough unless we are smaller. Unless there is less of us, we are not good enough.

Living by the girl code means living in a prison, a place where we try to keep ourselves small to fit in. If we wanted to invent a system to ensure that the world is not run by powerful women? We would raise them to fear the size of their bellies, to suck in their cheeks to make duck faces so they look thinner, to spend hours every day worrying that their bodies are not good enough to be in the world.

We live in that system.

I have a daughter who is ten as I write this. She is being raised in a generation of girls who wear *The Future is Female* emblazoned across their chests. This past summer, she attended a Girls Rock Math camp and bonded with other girls who dressed in combat leggings and colorful sneakers. Not one of her friends knows how to speak in girl code yet. Middle school and puberty are coming, however. Is this generation truly ready to stop being programmed by girl code?

I'm trying to break the code in myself so she doesn't copy what she sees in me.

I am fifty-two years old now. Instead of waiting for permission to love my own body only if it is small enough, I have surveyed what I am lucky enough to have, from my feet on the ground to the top of my head, and find joy in this body now.

Let's go back to it. Let me show you where it's strong instead.

Feet

My feet are sturdy. They're my base of power. And high heels hurt like hell when you wear them too long. I can't. I won't. I'm free to stomp around any way I want. I take long walks often, with friends and alone, up hills and down mountains. My legs have muscles. I will be walking well into my nineties. Walk with me.

Legs

My hips are birthing hips. I am balanced on them, deep in my pelvis, the seat of my power. I know how to dance from my hips, not from my shoulders or in awkward hand gestures. I know how to *move*. I don't give a crap anymore about shaving my legs. Now that I am nearing menopause, the hair is more sparse, but it's still there. I just don't examine it anymore.

Belly

My belly has grown a child. I grew a human being in my belly. Six-pack abs and hollowed-out spaces feel silly now. I can create life in me. Once you grow a child, it's time to stop worrying that your belly isn't perfect. My belly should be soft and rounded, with a pooch at the bottom where the muscles will never be taut again. This is how I am built.

Breasts

I had my breasts removed last year.

My mother and her three sisters have had breast cancer. After my first breast cancer scare I discovered I had a 93 percent chance of developing breast cancer at some point in my life. It was such an awful score that I made it into a joke for a full year. "I've always been a straight-A student!"

I opted for a double mastectomy without reconstruction. It never occurred to me to have a doctor build false breasts for me. I was done with pretending. The relief of not having men stare at my breasts first was second only to my relief of not having to worry about breast cancer anymore. A couple of days before the surgery, I threw a "so long, tatas!" party. A bunch of us women burned our bras in the parking lot. We celebrated.

It was one hell of a journey, and I'm stronger for the experience in ways that I'm still understanding.

And I love not having to wear a bra.

Arms

These arms were made for heavy lifting. You need help moving? I'm there. You need me to hold your crying child since the other child has run away across the street? I can do that. You need the biggest, warmest hug on a day when everything else feels grey? My arms are open.

Collarbone

I will not sacrifice the chance to love being in this body before it grows frail and breaks down because my collarbone does not show through my skin. When did bones become the template for beauty? All throughout history, in paintings and sculptures, women had curves and folds of flesh. This time of thinking we should starve ourselves for beauty is temporary. (And frankly, mostly white. So many black and Latina women seem to carry their flesh with far more grace than I ever have.)

Jawline

Every morning, I lather up with shaving cream that smells of mango and shave my neck, chin, and upper lip. After all these years, I still shave. I know a woman in my town who has a full beard. Good for her! But I still feel more comfortable with a smooth chin. When my daughter first asked what I was doing, I explained, "My body has a hormonal imbalance that means I grow some hair on my face." And she said, "Oh," then she went back to her happy playing. I turned back to the mirror and thought of how different my life could have been if I had said this to myself years ago.

Face

Makeup stopped making any sense to me years ago. However, I have developed a firm passion for bright-red lipstick. Who knew? I wash my face every morning with a goat's milk soap made by a farmer I know. I pat dry my face and dot on some lotion I bought at the drugstore, the inexpensive kind recommended by the dermatologist. There. My entire skincare regimen. People compliment me on my youthful glow often.

Ears

I'm so grateful I can hear the swell of music and the sound of the wind rustling through the trees in our yard. My ears work well.

Cheeks

When I smile, I can feel my cheeks rise to meet my eyes. That's when I know I'm fully in this moment of happiness.

Eyes

The technology for making glasses has reduced my lenses to a sliver around the frames. I stopped remembering that I used to hate myself in glasses until my daughter chose her first pair—bright purple—with the confidence she has for everything in life. No hint of feeling bad. She can see better now. So can I.

Hair

My hair is thinning on top. I spent the first four decades of my life with too much hair and now I have too little. Once, I thought that thinning hair only happened to men, but now I know that's not true. Women's hair gets thin too, far more often than is talked about in public. For a while, no matter how I combed it, I could see my scalp under the increasingly thin strands.

I started to feel the old despair rising up once again—*I'm not typical, not beautiful, not good enough*—and then I decided to stop it. I grabbed my husband's electric razor and took off a chunk of the hair I had been trying to grow again. *Maybe if it's longer and hits my shoulders, people won't notice the thinning on top.* There I went again, still rearranging parts of my body to make some of it look better and hide the rest. "Enough pretending," I heard myself say out loud. By mistake, I took a big chunk out of the back. So, when my husband returned home, I asked him to shave my head.

This was in early December, just after a certain election, when a mass of women were angry that a man who openly admitted to sexual harassment won the presidency. The notion of trying to conform to the standards of female beauty in a culture that expects us to be attractive to men like that? I wanted nothing to do with it. *Enough*, I said in my head as I bent down and let my husband shave off all my hair. (For the record, he thought this was pretty sexy.) I stood up and I could see my face, my wide eyes, my grey scalp. I felt free.

As I walked outside, I felt something I had not experienced before. Being bald, I could feel that my head—and thus my body—parted the air as I walked. Cool air streamed around my head, making space for me. I had never known that air was so palpable. For the first time, I felt it in my body: I am a being in the world, part of something much larger, not a single entity entirely dedicated to herself, in derision or in devotion.

I'm here.

I am so damned lucky.

THIS MOMENT, ENOUGH

I reach out my arm to turn off the alarm. Six in the morning. Feet on the floor. As I walk down the stairs in a quiet house, I'm struck again by the irony of me becoming the morning person. As a kid, I hit the snooze button on my alarm again and again, not wanting to start the day. When I lived in New York, I regularly stayed up until three or four in the morning, out dancing with friends, then coming home on the subway grinning. After Lucy was born I was forced to rise early, since she was wide awake and ready to start singing every day at five in the morning until she turned five. After Desmond arrived, however, I realized that early morning was the only sliver of time that was mine, entirely. So I started setting the alarm instead of wanting to steal a few more moments of sleep. I make the coffee and listen to the water start to burble through. I settle on the couch with a new thick book from the library. For thirty minutes, I am by myself, reading.

Usually Danny comes down next. Sometimes it's Lucy. Whoever it is, we have a hug, then talk about the day. Lucy puts a gluten-free bagel in the toaster. Danny reaches for coffee. Desmond runs down the stairs, full tilt, and jumps into my arms. Every morning, we snuggle. We started this when he was a baby, and this boy likes his routines. This might be my favorite moment of the day. Everyone awake but no need to go anywhere yet. Desmond cuddles in my arms while I rub his back and sing my modified version of a song from *Singin' in the Rain*: "Good morning, good morning. You've slept the whole night through. Good morning, good morning, to you." Then we put on the Beatles and start the day.

We eat breakfast, sing amen, and say our gratitude. Desmond squirms. Lucy reads her book. Danny and I laugh. Sometimes we're annoyed. It doesn't last long. We drink more coffee.

At one point in our lives, I gave up and accepted that from the moment I said it was time to go—shoes on, hair combed, and walking out the door—it would take at least a full hour to leave. *Oh look, Lucy found one of her graphic novels on the stairs and she sat down to read midstep. Desmond? Oh, you're in the kitchen making a drink with peanut butter, ranch dressing, and lemon juice? Nope, kiddo. It's time to go.* This three-ring circus is much calmer now. Danny was recently diagnosed with ADHD and because we realized he does best with clear structure and prep lists, I've taken the lead on keeping our household organized. The kids have chores, set to specific times on specific days. Saturday at ten o'clock? *Time to do your laundry, Lucy.* Early Friday evening, before we start movie night—put the gloves, shoes, and water bottles into each of the bags for sports or activities next week. When I waited for life to organize itself, our lives were a mess. I have become that mom who is regularly directing traffic and posting lists to the wall with schedules for the day. With less clutter, there are fewer distractions. From the time I say "Let's go!" to when we are in the car is less than fifteen minutes now.

On Sundays, we drive down the highway of our island, noticing the depth of blue in the water of the harbor. Sometimes it is raining. Usually we are listening to music—Stevie Wonder, Janelle Monae, or Lady Gaga (Lucy's request lately). We arrive at our fellowship hall and move toward the door.

Nearly six years ago, we joined our island's Unitarian fellowship. A friend with kids close in age told us one night about the services: Mary Oliver poems; Carl Sagan quotes; conversations about feeding our people; protests at the detention center in Tacoma; and ways to help the member who is on hospice for her stage IV cancer. I said to her, "Well, that all sounds great, but how much Jesus stuff is there?"

She laughed. "Honey, I'm a Jew. There's no Jesus stuff."

After my years of Buddhist work, I still sit meditation every day. However, with small children, I can no longer attend silent weekend retreats on a regular basis. We wanted a community, a place where we could find connection with people who were asking the big questions of life without the dogma of a specific religion. Danny was raised Catholic but he left the church. I had never been raised in a religion. We found ourselves trying to find a place for ritual and community, where our kids could learn about the world's religions too. We found that with the Unitarians. Every Sunday, we settle into the back of this modest hall, festooned with bouquets made with flowers from the members' gardens.

And together, we sing Elizabeth Norton and the Reverend Rebecca Parker's song:

"There is a love holding us. / There is a love holding all that we love. / There is a love, holding all. / We rest in this love."

We start with quotes and then a story for all ages. The kids gather around and listen to whomever is reading the book that day—sometimes it is me. We stand as one and sing the children out to their classes: "Go now in peace. Go now in peace. May the spirit of love surround you, everywhere, everywhere you may go." And our kids walk down to the building at the bottom of the hill with their teachers, to study Hinduism or Jainism or Islam. But mostly, they play and talk about their values. And Danny and I? We are free to sit with our community—without our kids asking for food or stepping on our feet. I look forward to this hour every week.

There are sermons and offerings and singing. However, my favorite fifteen minutes—perhaps of the entire week—is Joys and Concerns. We make space to hear each other's stories. Those who have something to share are invited to come forward, light a candle, and share something that is giving them joy or concern. Members voice joys about their time protesting at the detention center and letters from friends, and concerns about climate change, uncles injured in accidents, and the latest horrors of democracy. We all listen.

Our oldest member, Beryl, stands up. When she turned ninety-eight, we all sang to her. I organized a potluck of all her favorite recipes, based on the recipe box she gave me that year. She told me, "I won't be making these anymore. I figured you could enjoy them." She is almost one hundred but she still lives alone, drives herself to church on Sundays, and attends lectures and concerts. A few years ago, we worried when we didn't see her for a few weeks, but it turns out she had flown to meet friends on the Appalachian Trail. Beryl is absolutely who I want to be when I grow up.

She shuffles to the microphone, lights a candle, and turns to face us. "I'm so grateful to have made it this long. And I will tell you, from this distance, that how much money you have, the places you visit, the list of what you *should* do—none of it matters. All that matters is that you have your friends and your community. It's the only thing that stays. That is enough."

I have tears in my eyes, again.

At the coffee hour afterward, we sign up for meal trains, talk with our friends, and listen to people share their latest troubles or dreams. Every week, we leave with our hearts full, grateful for such a community.

When we go home, the kids play while Danny and I clean out the refrigerator. I put on Beethoven's Ninth Symphony. We make our shopping list as "Ode to Joy" rings out. Desmond enters the kitchen and plays along on his kazoo.

Lucy and I drop off Danny and Desmond at the soccer field and we go to the grocery store. We buy only what is on our list. Once in a while, I stop to show her the difference in prices between the brands with cartoons on the package and the ones in plain wrappers. I didn't learn how to keep a reasonable budget—and stick to it—until after our flour company failed. I won't let Lucy be so unaware. She grabs a bag of gluten-free flour for baking and I'm relieved that I will never have to sell ours again.

Back at home, we put away the groceries and Danny brines the chicken and sets it in the fridge. Then it's time for a hike in the woods. The kids complain that it's too cold out and too long of a walk, but this is not negotiable. Five minutes of driving and we are on a trail far away from houses. Ten minutes in and the kids are running, turning over leaves and looking for bugs. Danny and I walk hand in hand, watching them both, knowing how quickly they will outgrow us, drinking it all in.

When we return home, Danny puts the chicken in to roast, along with little blanched purple potatoes, spiky slices of romanesco, and fresh carrots. An hour later, our dear friends Tita and John arrive for dinner. We sit at the dining room table, the kids teasing John, who is like their enormously tall uncle. They eat, then run upstairs to play. I put my elbows on the table and lean into the conversation. It's number 7,328 of the many, many talks between us over the past twenty-six years.

Tita and John take their dishes to the sink—they insist—and we hug. The kids run down the stairs to fling themselves at John and hug Tita's legs. We wave goodbye, then turn to do the dishes. Lucy and Desmond empty the dishwasher. I rinse the dishes. Danny puts away the food. We have Chopin playing, some quiet-down music before bed. Our kitchen and our home are pretty small, so we fit in there snugly. But we're all there, together.

"Lucy, lay out your clothes for tomorrow. Desmond get your butt in here, little guy! Time for your bath. Do you want Spider-Man in there with you?" At one point, Lucy is running to our bathroom to turn on the shower, and a naked little boy is chasing after her, giggling. I look up at Danny at the end of the hall and we both start laughing. There will be wrangling soon, to get Desmond to sleep, and coax Lucy to dry her hair and brush it so I don't have to deal with a thousand tangles tomorrow. We still have awhile before they are both asleep, before we can lie in bed together, watch a food travel show, make plans for the week, and talk about the day.

In this moment, however, we can see it in each other. We both have enough.

• • •

L ately I have been thinking about the moment when I sat meditation in New York, vulnerable in the front of the room, crying.

I cried because I went deep inside my loneliness. In my mind's eye, I stepped back into the house where I had been raised and saw my young self being aggressively questioned by my mother. I reached out my hand and offered an exit to that scared kid who didn't know when the darkness would end. The adult me didn't say a word. I held out my hand and she took it. We walked out of the house together.

For years, I thought that was enough. I left that house. My adult self helped my little self to leave. I was free.

Now, I know that I need to do more. I need to welcome in that little girl. She's out there, maybe not knowing she has a home. On a Sunday evening, as the kids are taking their baths, I go outside in the darkness and find her hand. I squeeze that cold little hand and keep holding it as I lead her into our home. When I open the door, she is dazzled by the light. She doesn't see the clutter. She doesn't see the to-do lists or the shabby carpeting. All she sees is light. I lead her upstairs, where we stand, side by side, and watch, together, as Desmond runs through the hall giggling, and Lucy—who is two years older than that little girl and far more free—laughs and dances her way to the bathroom.

We watch as Danny, my darling husband, gently puts our son into the warm water of the bath. They play superheroes and splash around. Lucy belts out a song in the shower, one she has been singing in rehearsals all week for her musical theater performance. We stand, that little one and I, hand in hand, taking it all in.

And then I kneel down on the top of the stairs and I put my arms around her. I can feel her fall into me, sobbing. And I rub her back and hug her close. *I know, I know,* I murmur to her. *I remember. But this. This is what awaits you. Life will find you, little one. And you're going to love it one day. The darkness will fade away. You're going to liberate yourself. You don't know your own strength yet.*

Carry this with you. This light, this singing, this perfectly ordinary day. It will be yours.

And it will be enough.

ACKNOWLEDGMENTS

No one writes a book alone. I am grateful for all the people who listened to my story, thus giving me the courage to share it.

Thank you to Tita, who was the first person in the world to hear my story when I was 29 years old. My friend, you made me feel understood.

Thank you to Sharon, who has been there since 1982, for making me laugh and listening to me wonder. Always, my friend.

Thank you to Gabe, Margo, Melinda, Meri, Sam, Tamiko, Tina, and Trish for always listening. Thanks for being my people.

Thank you to all the brave women writers who told their stories before me: Maya Angelou, Heather Armstrong, Brené Brown, Roxane Gay, Kat Kinsman, Michelle Obama, Maggie O'Farrell, Oprah, and Virginia Woolf.

And to the wonderful people of the weird town of Vashon—I am so happy to know you.

Thank you to Dr. G, whose wisdom sustained me through some years of questioning.

Thank you to my parents and my brother. Those were difficult times. We have not healed yet. Maybe someday.

Thank you to Stacey Glick, who chose to be my agent when I had only been writing a food blog for six months. Thank you for believing in me.

Thank you to the incredible team at Sasquatch and beyond for your helpful and meaningful contributions: Jessyca Murphy, Rachelle Longé McGhee, Nikki Sprinkle, Jenny Abrami, Molly Woolbright, Jill Saginario, Bryce de Flamand, Daniel Germain, and Abby Weintraub.

And to Susan Roxborough, a multitude of graces and gratitude. You are the editor I always longed to have. You supported my writing and my voice. And you hacked the hell out of the essays that didn't work. This book would not be this book without you.

To my darling children, Lucy and Desmond, who teach me and make me laugh every day. Being your mama is the most important job of my life.

And to Danny, who is love. As Tita says, you are the best thing that has ever happened to me. Thank you for listening to every single essay in this book before I hit send. And thank you for being you.

And to all who are reading? Let's work together to help find our own definitions of enough and be brave enough to share them. We could change the world.

ABOUT THE AUTHOR

SHAUNA M. AHERN has been writing all her life. For more than a decade, she was best known for her food writing. She is the author of four critically acclaimed cookbooks, including *Gluten-Free Girl Every Day*, which won a 2014 James Beard Book Award. Shauna's work has been published and recognized by the *New York Times*, *Bon Appétit*, the *Guardian*, and the *Washington Post*. Shauna is a personal essayist at heart. She lives on a rural island off Seattle, Washington, with her husband, Daniel, and their two children.